Poor Americans:
How the White Poor Live

*trans*action books

Poor Americans:
How the White Poor Live

Edited by

MARC PILISUK AND PHYLLIS PILISUK

*trans***action** books

Distributed by
Aldine Publishing Company

The essays in this book originally appeared
in *trans***action** magazine

TA Book 24
Library of Congress Catalog Number 79-133309

Contents

Preface

However diverse their attitudes and interpretations may sometimes be, social scientists are now entering a period of shared realization that the United States—both at home and abroad—has entered a crucial period of transition. Indeed, the much burdened word "crisis" has now become a commonplace among black militants, Wall Street lawyers, housewives, and even professional politicians.

For the past eight years, *trans*action magazine has dedicated itself to the task of reporting the strains and conflicts within the American system. But the magazine has done more than this. It has pioneered in social programs for changing the society, offered the kind of analysis that has permanently restructured the terms of the "dialogue" between peoples and publics, and offered the sort of prognosis that makes for real alterations in social and political policies directly affecting our lives.

The work done in the pages of *trans*action has crossed professional boundaries. This represents much more than simple cross-disciplinary "team efforts." It embodies rather a recognition that the social world cannot be easily carved into neat academic areas. That, indeed, the study of the experience of blacks in American ghettos, or the manifold uses and abuses of agencies of law enforcement, or the sorts of overseas policies that lead to the celebration of some dictatorships and the condemnation of others, can best be examined from many viewpoints and from the vantage points of many disciplines.

This series of books clearly demonstrates the superiority of starting with real world problems and searching out practical solutions, over the zealous guardianship of professional boundaries. Indeed, it is precisely this approach that has elicited enthusiastic support from leading American social scientists for this new and dynamic series.

The demands upon scholarship and scientific judgment are particularly stringent, for no one has been untouched by the current situation. Each essay republished in these volumes bears the imprint of the author's attempt to communicate his own experience of the crisis. Yet, despite the sense of urgency these papers exhibit, the editors feel that many have withstood the test of time, and match in durable interest the best of available social science literature. This collection of *trans*action articles, then, attempts to address itself to immediate issues without violating the basic insights derived from the classical literature in the various fields of social science.

The subject matter of these books concerns social changes that have aroused the longstanding needs and present-day anxieties of us all. These changes are in organizational life styles, concepts of human ability and intelligence, changing patterns of norms and morals, the relationship of social conditions to physical and biological environments, and in the status of social science with national policy making.

The dissident minorities, massive shifts in norms of social conduct, population explosions and urban expansions, and vast realignments between nations of the world of recent years do not promise to disappear in the seventies. But the social scientists involved as editors and authors of this *trans*action series have gone beyond observation of these critical areas, and have entered into the vital and difficult tasks of explanation and interpretation. They have defined issues in a way making solutions possible. They have provided answers as well as asked the right questions. Thus, this series should be conceived as the first collection dedicated not to highlighting social problems alone, but to establishing guidelines for social solutions based on the social sciences.

THE EDITORS
*trans*action

Poor Americans:
An Introduction

MARC PILISUK/PHYLLIS PILISUK

Social problems go in and out of vogue as a result of both cultural fads and political processes. The alliance in the Democratic party between its southern factions and its other constituencies was jarred by the civil rights movement of the early 1960s, and the impact continued to be felt as young activists decided to bypass the local discriminating barber shop in favor of the restaurant chain and went on to voter registration in the terror-filled counties of rural Mississippi. The Democratic split, averted in 1960 by Lyndon Johnson's nomination as Vice-President, was later healed, temporarily, by a politically astute transfer of the issue from race to poverty. In 1964 and 1965 a host of monographs, anthologies, conferences and proceedings appeared, all of which rediscovered the other America. Even the Republicans contributed Barry Goldwater as a foil in 1964, and thereby assisted in the building of a new united front behind Lyndon Johnson's budding War on Poverty. SDS and the corporations together campaigned for

Johnson and an air of optimism prevailed. People began to believe that cold war hysteria and cold war budgets might soon be replaced by a crusade to put an end to the indignity of human poverty.

Meanwhile, however, the years of cloak and dagger politics on the part of the United States in Burma, Thailand, Indonesia, Laos and Vietnam were beginning to bear bitter fruit. The convert manipulation and support of feudal regimes, the buildup of military forces (secretly in evasion of the Geneva Accords) was failing, and the money and effort needed to wage war on domestic poverty were needed to cover the failures abroad. The many proverty programs went on, but now without the commitment of a "war." Instead a series of starts and demonstrations held out hopes that were never really fulfilled. It is in the competition for scarce resources that the poor, now definitely declared to exist, have emerged as factions. The Appalachian ex-miner, the unskilled and underemployed worker, and ADC mother and her children, the aged, the disabled, blacks, browns, native Americans present different problems and different loci of organizational pressure upon the system. One last effort to reunite these factions to launch a real war on poverty disappeared in the mud of Resurrection City in 1968.

We are now in an era in which the structural problems underlying most of American poverty are being ignored in favor of low-cost patchwork that leaves the social structure intact. The programs have been in effect long enough so that we now know that both the economics and the culture of poverty are resistant to change. This resistance, while apparent enough among those of the poor who are reluctant to give up certain psychosocial and economic dependencies, is most striking, however, among the haves who are reluctant to give up their advantages. In any case, it is time to take stock of the separate groups of poor people and the efforts that have been made to help them. What have we learned about poverty, about our society and our abilities to change it?

Poverty for most middle-class Americans is associated with the black, the chicano, the Puerto Rican, and the Indian. The most vivid portrayals of poverty in novels and in the media have been set mainly in black ghettos. But the poverty of minority groups still leaves half the American poor, or more than 12 million Caucasians, to be considered. While many of the problems of poverty in America are generic, i.e., independent of race, the emphasis here will be upon the poverty of white Americans.

The white poor are not linked to one another by any sense of comparable heritage, common victimization or ethnicity. They are but the remaining classification after the racial minorities have been counted and even within this classification it is probably impossible to identify subgroups that do not overlap with the minority poor. Nevertheless, the categories which appear useful to us are the following:

☐ Unskilled or partly skilled rejects of industrial change. This includes the vast number of ex-coal miners, particularly from the Appalachian regions. It includes the workers displaced when local industries failed or relocated. Studies show that large numbers of these once stable lower middle-class persons are unable to relocate. Many of the group, over 40 and with families, are still struggling years after their plant closings for the most meagre of temporary jobs. They are people whose possessions and debts combine with the lack of job opportunity to force a demoralizing downgrading of their sense of worth.

☐ A partly overlapping category of white poor is Harrington's economic underclass. They are the holders of temporary and menial jobs, in hotels, laundries, kitchens, furnace rooms, nonunionized factories and hospitals. They

shift rapidly, are not in any organization, and are easily
exploited by labor racketeers and by management blood-
suckers. The group is significant for it points to people who
do, at times, hold jobs but can find in them neither status,
security, nor even the income to live in minimal decency.
The minimum wage law still has large loopholes that permit such exploitation.

☐ About a third of the destitute migratory farm workers
are white. A similar proportion of farm-owning poor still
exist on dilapidated farms in depressed farming areas that
have changed little since the years of the great depression.
The farm rejects, particularly from the South, who are
driven to the northern cities to compete for scarce, low-
paying jobs, become part of the urban underclass.

☐ Retirement in dignity is still the exception rather than
the rule in the United States. The elderly face the dual
problem of inability to work through illness and of being
pressured out of the job market. Half the aged in the United
States live below the minimum standards required for
decent survival. Many are victims of relocation from a once
familiar neighborhood to isolation in cheap rooming houses
or old hotels. While they are the most likely to be sick, the
poorest often cannot even pay the small fees required of
them for medicare coverage. The poorest of the poor are
those least affected by social security or any other pensions
or retirement funds. Widows, who predominate in the over
75 age group, are particularly vulnerable to extreme isolation and lack of funds. Even among those covered by
traditional social security there is often great deprivation.
The breakdown of the extended family frequently makes
life for an older person with his offspring a burden to both.
Yet "making it" socially in a household of one's own requires economic outlays to cover services, transportation,
telephone, as well as food. It is no wonder then that state
mental hospitals and makeshift nursing homes provide

major centers of custodial care for this category of the poor.
□ The physically handicapped, the mentally retarded and the emotionally ill are probably over-represented in white poverty. The white person not so handicapped has always enjoyed relatively greater opportunity in education and jobs than members of minority groups. Those who remain poor, more frequently than among racial minorities, are often people who are unable to use such opportunities. In this group we should include some drug addicts and a large portion of the alcoholics and sometime alcoholic derelicts of skid row. The entire category of physically or mentally needy exposes several major problems of the social order: 1) the failure to provide essential services to many, 2) the failure to provide adequately for those who cannot work and, underlying these, 3) the refusal of society to sanction the idea that people are worth something other than what they can earn in the economic market.
□ Welfare recipients are poor. It is true that the poorest of the poor do not get any assistance. They are too ignorant, too badly handicapped or too beaten by the system to press for what is due them. It is those who know how to operate within the system who take such risks as wearing a girdle to conceal pregnancy and thus retain an extra month of unemployment compensation to furnish a crib for the child. A shrewd mother hides her male acquaintances to get AFDC, which is in any case pitifully inadequate. Budgetary allocations under AFDC often fall significantly below even the various Labor Department and local minimum subsistance figures. It is just a mistake to think of those who are covered as being able to survive financially. In one study a majority of the AFDC mothers questioned felt they fed their children inadequately. In all the sample there was no fruit, only little of the most inferior cuts of meat and vegetables were rare. For many, food stamps required a cost outlay at the wrong time of the month. Rent and

⨉ utility bills take the giant share of an AFDC check, leaving almost nothing for clothing, transportation or any family treats, such as birthday presents. The choices between lowered electric bills and leaving the light on to scare off rats, between paying carfare for all the children when taking one to the clinic or leaving the others unattended, or between paying an overdue heating bill or buying children shoes, all are matters of fact in the lives of those of our poor for whom welfare does provide.

☐ Young people have little earning capacity on the marketplace. In poor families the teenager becomes a competitor for temporary menial jobs which lead to nothing but sustained poverty, if and when they are available. This problem has been most serious with minority youth. Increasingly, however, there is a new group of young people, the self-made poor, who have deserted their middle-class homes and what they see as the shallow plastic culture of their parents to make it on their own in the counterculture. Many of these young people have cut off ties with parents and they would not work regularly for a bureaucracy even if such work were available. The freedom they sought has been curtailed by the straight society, the police and the hard dealers. Voluntarily at first, but as they move from unstable commune to crash pad, inevitably, they are poor and increasingly fatalistic.

The young hip poor person is poor because he rejects aspects of white middle-class culture, its hypocritical condemnation of drugs and violence, its achievement emphasis, its rationalism, its materialism, its denial of pleasurable experience, and the self-estranging character of the work it provides. Alienated youth living on their own are not all interminably poor. Some have contact with a parent who is psychologically and geographically close enough to bail them out of emergencies. Others have been in the mainstream long enough to have mastered the prerequisite skills for reentry into the world of colleges and jobs. But for many the cultural bridge has burned. They have never identified with their broken homes, and many have become veterans of surviving on the street by the age of sixteen. For this latter group, their rejection of the technocracy may still be a matter of choice; their poverty, however, is there to stay.

The hippies are a most provocative group since the aspects of middle class culture they intentionally reject are precisely the aspects that poverty programs seek to graft on to the poor in an effort to make them employable. The values of the counter culture have a certain intrinsic worth are are bound to spread into a more generalized repeal of the Protestant ethic. The question for antipoverty warriors becomes whether poverty is to be the price of those who reject or refuse to assimilate into the mainstream culture or will adequate income and vital services be available to those who live and think differently?

We have selected the essays in this volume to describe various aspects of white poverty in America. Only a few of the poverty groupings we have identified are covered and only two attempt a phenomenological view of an impoverished state of existence, one of an Appalachia resident and one of a Berkeley hippie. Others are included to elaborate upon the subcultural supports of these groups, which are often mechanisms for poverty maintenance. Some articles are included to suggest the relative position of the poor in the larger society.

Both the culture of the poor and their position in the larger society will be discussed in our second volume on poor Americans, which describes the dynamics of change. Change is not easily come by and both the cultures of poor people and the intransigence of the social order have been blamed for the slow rate of progress. For convenience we have separated three components of the change process: indigenous social action, professional and paraprofessional services, and social policy.

Our working model of the change process with regard to

domestic poverty, begins with the assumption that there is no magical lever to push, no Rosetta Stone that enables us to decipher the secret of how to eradicate the disgrace of poverty. Rather, change comes about through a comprehensible, if unpleasant, process which if understood may sometimes be hastened. The first fact to be considered in this process is that, with the exception of certain pockets of extremely isolated individuals, poor people do live in more or less viable and more or less supportive subcultural arrangements. To the extent that the poor must take sustained action in any program designed for them, that program will have to take into account the needs fulfilled by their existing beliefs and interaction patterns. When the values of these existing arrangements or subcultures are recognized, it becomes easier to comprehend the reluctance of the individual poor person to cut his ties, change his vocabulary and manners and reach out to some program which, though it may be called "Horizons Unlimited," actually offers him little more than the chance to be competitive at the lower level of the labor market.

The poor do have an importance, however, in the dynamics of change. It is a role that requires a strengthening of the ties of their own communities around issues of common concern. Through collective protest, and perhaps through no other route, the poor can open the channels through which they may be heard. The effort itself can be personally productive for the activists. A mentally healthy person must be able to take action toward goals that have positive meaning for himself and his group. Social action creates an opportunity to break out of the resignation and despair that are frequent components of the generalized culture of poverty. Indigenous action also provides the only genuine pressure that poor people can bring to bear on the political process. There is, however, an attribute of poor subcultures that offers both a potential for radical organization and a source of ambiguity regarding the direction such action may take. Oscar Lewis makes the observation:

A critical attitude toward some of the values and institutions of the dominant classes, hatred of the police, mistrust of the government and those in high position, and a cynicism which extends even to the church gives the culture of poverty a counter quality and a potential for being used in political movements aimed against the existing social order (Lewis, *Scientific American*, 1966).

How this potential is used depends in part on the roles of the professional and of indigenous leadership. The professional has several roles in the change process. The most difficult and perhaps the most important is to permit communication across the cultures. To do this we must learn to listen to the anguish and the anger. We must be able to understand the cultural symbols that give meaning to the lives of somewhat alien communities. It is a task that cannot be done without guides whose origins among the poor subcultures make them capable of reaching out to clients in ways rarely available to the typical professional. For this reason the paraprofessional takes on increased importance both as conveyer of communication from the poor and as a means for delivery of services.

Since no currently available services terminate the client's poverty, the professional and paraprofessional must serve in nontraditional ways. Advocacy is an important example. No therapist in a mental health center or physician in a clinic, no welfare worker or teacher's aide can serve adequately in a community of poverty without becoming an advocate for more services of higher quality, for greater participation and control in the hands of the community. Even professional research should be engaged more often on behalf of, rather than simply on, the client population.

There could be great advantage in letting the poor know as much about the prediction and control of the powerful men who are gatekeepers of their destinies as these gatekeepers are continually learning from social scientists about the behavior of the disadvantaged. We see the professional here as helping to direct the frustration from unmet needs to the powers most crucial in determining policy.

So far we have been dealing with *community* pressure and *community* change. This is the only locus of pressure that the poor communities can generate. Yet American poverty cannot be eradicated on a community level. Economic impoverishment is a product, not an accident of an economic system that functions well for some but distributes incomes most inequitably. The system is pervasive. Technological displacement, opposition to welfare for the poor, tax inequities, dependence upon unstable war industry, the use of efficiency criteria without regard to human costs, all are matters of national policy. Patterns of support for services are both state and national matters. Structural unemployment represents the wiping out not of certain jobs but of certain classes of jobs for which no amount of poor people's mobility or local organization may compensate. Hence, national action is needed. The professional and the reform-minded legislator have a role here in the design of social policy. There are dangers and limits in this role. The dangers lie in creating policy that fails to respect the rights of choice of the poor person and in destroying his culture without recognition of the needs it serves. Plans to draft all 1-Y rejects and give them a chance through military socialization are of this order. The Army's Project 100,000 is a similar model of resocialization by coercion. A guaranteed income, in contrast, could eliminate a good deal of squalor without demanding such a price.

The limits of legislative action are revealed by an understanding of which pressures get enacted into law and which do not, and by an appreciation of the interests that block threatening inroads. Professionals and agency administrators prevented the new careers program from turning over to non-professional workers the many aspects of professional work and supervisory responsibility that could well be performed more cheaply by less highly trained people. It is the relatively stable subsidies allotted to defense industries, large farmers, oil companies, military and intelligence agencies that preclude subsidies for people who are unable to obtain a decent income through work. The professional policy planner and the reform legislator work within confines too restricted by compelling priorities to eradicate poverty. What they can do effectively is work at the fringes to change the balance among these subsidized priorities. It is our belief that at least some of these legislative actions must be geared to the creation and maintenance of bases for continued pressure from poor communities, just as the contracts to defense industries provide the funds for their lobbyists. This loop from poor community, to social action, to helping professional, to social policy and back again to poor community is our model for the dynamics of changing poverty in America.

There is hope that certain poor people will escape their ghettos and move on the road to middle-class standards of living and perhaps to the shallowness of middle-class existence. There is less hope that our society will permit poverty to disappear. The various subcultures of white poverty —ex-miners, the street gangs, the disabled, the aged— cannot even afford the luxury of the black illusion of a separate society. These poor groups are part of the same social order in which the distributive process gives some men great wealth and power at the expense of others who are poor and powerless. White poverty and white affluence are symptoms of the same disease. Pockets of isolation and despair belong to the same order as great concentrations of political, ecomonic and police power. Both must be made to surrender to a more humane image of society.

FURTHER READING:

"Budgeting and the Poor: A View from the Bottom" by S. Barr, (*Public Welfare*, October 1965), pp. 246-250.

"The Power of the Poor" by W. C. Haggstrom, in Frank Reissman, Jerome Cohen and Arthur Pearl, *The Mental Health of the Poor*, (Glencoe: Free Press, 1964).

"Is There a Culture of Poverty?" by Elizabeth Herzog, in Hanna H. Meissner (ed.) *Affluent Society*. (New York: Harper and Row, 1966).

The Other America by Michael Harrington (New York: Macmillan Company, 1964).

"The Betrayal of the American Poor" by Michael Harrington (*The Atlantic*, January 1970, pp, 71-74).

"Life on ADC: Budgets of Despair" by C. Lebeaux, (*New University Thought*, 1963, *3*, 26-35).

The Children of Sanchez by Oscar Lewis (New York: Random House, 1961).

"The Culture of Poverty," by Oscar Lewis (*Scientific American, 1966, 215, 16.*)

How the White Poor Live

MARC PILISUK/PHYLLIS PILISUK

The essays in this book attempt to describe some aspects of a life of poverty for some poor white groups. Many of the critical issues regarding these descriptions have been raised by Oscar Lewis in his various discussions of the culture of poverty. A culture is a pattern of beliefs, feelings and behavior, which hangs together. The utility of the culture of poverty concept lies in pointing to elements of a life style, frequently, but not always accompanying long term economic impoverishment. Economic impoverishment leads to a host of adjustments to hardship. Lewis, in other writings on the topic, however, makes clear that he is not referring to a deficit culture:

> ...poverty in modern nations is not only a state of economic deprivation, of disorganization or of the absence of something. It is also something positive in the sense that it has a structure, a rationale and defense mechanism without which the poor could hardly carry on. In short, it is a way of life, remarkably stable and

13

persistent, passed down from generation to generation along family lines. The culture of poverty has its own modalities and destructive social and psychological consequences (*Children of Sanchez*).

These consequences are then enumerated to show that this culture includes not only the feeling of marginality, despair and inferiority that are perfectly realistic for a group that cannot achieve socially designated values and goals, but also an attempt to cope with such feelings. The coping is by a more concretized personal outlook emphasizing the present and allowing more room for spontaneity, for expression of affect, for more magical resolutions in their religion. The question of whether this culture of poverty is sufficiently well integrated to be properly considered a culture is of more than academic interest. If a real culture is present, efforts toward purely economic uplift will have to be made to fit into the cultural pattern if they are to be accepted. Moreover, if the negative aspects of the culture, the sense of helplessness and not belonging, are the target, then money may not be sufficient to produce change.

There are two critical features missing from most descriptions of the generalized culture of poverty. These are, first, the sense of belonging to a cultural entity, a sense of allegiance to some group within which one shares beliefs and practices. The second deficiency lies in detailed descriptions of the roles and interaction patterns in the culture. It is sometimes claimed that the urban poor live as isolated individuals unbound by any sense of community even to others who live in relative proximity. Most frequently the isolation is not complete and reactions to impoverishment are knit into the cultural fabric. There is, however, a distinction between a more tenacious but adaptive cultural accommodation to poverty and a set of prevalent individual reactions to hopelessness. The article by Robert Coles describes well a true culture in the Appalachians. It is despairing, heart-rending, but not without important psychological and social strengths. It suggests a need, often disregarded in poverty and job training programs, to respect the strengths of the culture of poor people.

In urban settings cultural integration is weak for rich and poor alike. The shared values and social ties that bind people are either absent or exist in a very frail form at all income levels. But the opportunities for escape through socially sanctioned voluntary groupings are severely limited by poverty. The money for dues, carfare, the right clothes and the babysitter is just not there. But groups not socially sanctioned tend to emerge. The article on white gangs and on the serpent handling religions are interesting in this respect. For poor white urban youth, the larger culture provides no basis for positive identity. But the gang does. It provides an alternative status system, the definition of a turf, the admiration for fighting prowess or for the successful dealer or thief, the corner store with its adult figure who cares, and so forth. Where the culture of poverty was incomplete and not truly a viable culture for these people they have created a subcultural accomodation that, at least for a time, makes life bearable. Similarly, the serpent handlers, among the very poorest and most marginal of a generally poor area, have provided an age-graded subcultural accommodation that gives people the recognition denied them elsewhere. These are accommodations to poverty that are fraught with danger. Still, they do provide enough basis for the sense of worth that they may outweigh the lure of alternatives to forsake the clique and enter the mainstream of society at the lowest and least attractive rungs.

Ordinarily, poor subcultures just grow. They are not intentionally created by their members nor selectively joined by jealous outsiders. The counterculture of alienated young people represents a departure from this general rule. "Becky and the Telegraph Avenue Life Style" describes who the alienated young people are, why they come to the various centers of hip existence and what they find there.

⨯ Skid Row presents perhaps the extreme of isolated impoverishment in the cities. Pitman's article on "Homeless Men" suggests a life in which there is virtually no supporting clique to assure any sense of personal validity. For such men the measure of life's value may be seen in the frequency with which they are faced with the choice of spending weeks or months in jail as the alternative to paying a fine. For them the defensive accommodations to poverty, such as drunkenness, are less illustrative of a culture of poverty and more indicative of a severe, shattered ego. Skid Row, like the geriatrics ward of a state hospital, is a dumping ground for those unprotected even by the culture of poverty.

The way in which schools support the cycle of poverty is well illustrated by Estelle Fuchs in "How Teachers Help Children Fail." Slum schools first socialize their teachers into accepting as inevitable the inadequacies of the learning environment they provide. The teacher is then urged to pigeonhole children at the earliest grades into fast learners or slow learners. Equipped with the perspective that it is the child or his background which is deficient, such teachers prepare the children to be failures, as they will indeed be in a social or financial sense. Slum children are doomed by this philosophy of failure to be noncompetitive in the job market and, thus, to continue another generation of poverty.

Migrant farm labor is a more common form of institutionalized poverty among racial minorities than among poor whites. Among chicanos the heritage of La Raza offers some sense of community that prevents total alienation, if not deep feelings of economic waste and despair.

Poor black and white migrants, however, are reduced to an identity as part of the crew. But the crew (which is the unit by which a crew manager delivers farm labor) is not a unit geared to generating any sense of individual value. Rather, as Friedland's article suggests, the habits of treating migrants as low-grade rental machinery are so deeply engrained as to be perpetuated even where more humane farm management could be *less* costly to the farm employer. Farmers who employ migrant labor are perhaps not the most progressive capitalists in matters of consideration for their employees. The article does, however, raise an interesting question of how much the more enlightened industrialists do to keep their employees economically afloat. When the UAW proposed to Ford Motor Company that its older members be permitted to take a voluntary layoff so that newer workers could stay on, the company refused. The reason for Ford's refusal was that supplementary unemployment compensation for an old timer costs more than for a new worker. Once again the social conscience of the corporation surrendered to the profit motive. The other question raised in the article on farm labor is one that relates to our second volume, on solutions to poverty. Even at its most elastic, the efficiency criterion just does not do the job in providing jobs for people. The aged, the handicapped and the undereducated may or may not offer compensatory economic advantage to the potential employer. Similarly, the mothers of one-parent families who need reduced hours and child care facilities if employment is to help them, are, in purely financial terms, a bad bet. By requiring competitive marketability for stable employment, the system generates poverty.

Anselm Strauss documents the grossly inadequate medical services available to poor people. A poverty of services is just as much a part of a life in poverty as an absence of income. Rural Cuba has greater accessibility to doctors

than most poor sections of the United States. We might
have chosen dental care, education, welfare services, legal
services or housing. The picture is the same and so are
the reasons. The reasons include professionalism, the insistence by those charged with delivering the service that
the client play (or pay) the part on terms set forth by the
professional, terms that secure the professional's authority,
status and sense of importance. A second reason lies in the
assumption that the bulwarks of our system of services,
(guaranteed federal loans to builders and buyers, schooling
in overcrowded mass educational units, insurance to cover
skyrocketing medical costs, the compromising public
defender) can be tuned to the needs of poor people by minor
and low cost reforms. Every indication is that major re-
design of the system of services (at great cost) in needed.

It is the failure of services to meet basic needs that
accentuates the feeling among poverty subcultures of not
belonging. This feeling is a mirror image of the fact that
the system of services do not belong to them, which has
great implications for the importance of participation and
control in the design of services.

The article on public dependency indicates an underlying
value accommodation which transposes for us the question
of how to get people off welfare rolls. It suggests that so
great is the interdependence among parts of our technological society that we all are, in effect, recipients of the
dole. As such, the recipient of welfare, who still accounts
for less than half of the poor, is not parasitic but rather
symbiotic to the society, as are most of us. While economic
measures can and must be used to guarantee both adequate
minimum levels of income and essential services above the
subsistence line, this should be done with an eye toward
increasing the options available to the various poverty
cultures. We must beware of the subtle ways in which
images of public dependence are frequently used to

rationalize programs that seek to homogenize or otherwise destroy the subcultural strengths (including the insistence upon participation in planning) that some impoverished groups have developed.

The Culture of Poverty

OSCAR LEWIS

I want to take this opportunity to clear up some possible misunderstanding concerning the idea of a "culture of poverty." I would distinguish sharply between impoverishment and the culture of poverty. Not all people who are poor necessarily live in or develop a culture of poverty. For example, middle-class people who become impoverished do not automatically become members of the culture of poverty, even though they may have to live in the slums for a while. Similarly, the Jews who lived in poverty in eastern Europe did not develop a culture of poverty because their tradition of literacy and their religion gave them a sense of identification with Jews all over the world. It gave them a sense of belonging to a community which was united by a common heritage and common religious beliefs.

In the introduction to *The Children of Sanchez*, I listed approximately 50 traits which constitute what I call the culture of poverty. Although poverty is only one of the many traits which, in my judgment, go together, I have used it to name the total system because I consider it terribly important. However, the other traits, and especially the psychological and ideological ones, are also important and I should like to elaborate on this a bit.

[The people in the culture of poverty have a strong feeling of marginality, of helplessness, of dependency, of not belonging. They are like aliens in their own country, convinced that the existing institutions do not serve their interests and needs. Along with this feeling of powerlessness is a widespread feeling of inferiority, of personal unworthiness. This is true of the slum dwellers of Mexico City, who do not constitute a distinct ethnic or racial group and do not suffer from racial discrimination. In the United States the culture of poverty of the Negroes has the additional disadvantage of racial discrimination.

[People with a culture of poverty have very little sense of history. They are a marginal people who know only their own troubles, their own local conditions, their own neighborhood, their own way of life. Usually, they have neither the knowledge, the vision nor the ideology to see the similarities between their problems and those of others like themselves elsewhere in the world. In other words, they are not class conscious, although they are very sensitive indeed to status distinctions. When the poor become class conscious or members of trade union organizations, or when they adopt an internationalist outlook on the world they are, in my view, no longer part of the culture of poverty although they may still be desperately poor.

The idea of a culture of poverty that cuts across different societies enables us to see that many of the problems we think of as distinctively our own or distinctively Negro problems (or that of any other special racial or ethnic group), also exist in countries where there are no ethnic groups involved. It also suggests that the elimination of physical poverty as such may not be enough to eliminate the culture of poverty which is a whole way of life. One can speak readily about wiping out poverty; but to wipe out a culture or subculture is quite a different matter, for it raises the basic question of our respect for cultural differences.

Middle-class people, and this certainly includes most social scientists, tend to concentrate on the negative aspects of the culture of poverty; they tend to have negative feelings about traits such as an emphasis on the present and a neglect of the future, or on concrete as against abstract orientations. I do not intend to idealize or romanticize the culture of poverty. As someone has said, "It is easier to praise poverty than to live it." However, we must not overlook some of the positive aspects that may flow from these traits. Living immersed in the present may develop a capacity for spontaneity, for the enjoyment of the sensual, the indulgence of impulse, which is too often blunted in our middle-class future-oriented man. Perhaps it is this reality of the moment that middle-class existentialist writers are so desperately trying to recapture, but which the culture of poverty experiences as a natural, everyday phenomena. The frequent use of violence certainly provides a ready outlet for hostility, so that people in the culture of poverty suffer less from repression than does the middle class.

In this connection, I should also like to take exception to the trend in some studies to identify the lower class almost exclusively with vice, crime and juvenile delinquency, as if most poor people were thieves, beggars, ruffians, murderers or prostitutes. Certainly, in my own experience in Mexico, I found most of the poor decent, upright, courageous and lovable human beings. I believe it was the novelist Fielding who wrote, "The sufferings of the poor are indeed less observed than their misdeeds."

It is interesting that much the same ambivalence in the

evaluation of the poor is reflected in proverbs and in literature. On the positive side, the following serve as typical:

"Blessed be ye poor: for yours is the kingdom of God," (*Luke*, 6:20).

"The poor are the proteges of the Gods." (Menander, *The Lady of Leucas*, c. 330 B.C.)

"It is life near the bone, where it is sweetest." (H. D. Thoreau, *Walden*, Ch. 18.)

"The poor man alone, When he hears the poor moan From a morsel a morsel will give." (Thomas Holcraft, *Gaffer Gray.*)

"Yes! in the poor man's garden grow
Far more than herbs and flowers,
Kind thoughts, contentment, peace of mind,
And joy for weary hours."
(Mary Howitt, *The Poor Man's Garden.*)

"Poverty! Thou source of human art,
Thou great inspirer of the poet's song!"
(Edward Moore, *Hymn to Poverty.*)

"Few, save the poor, feel for the poor."
(Letitia Elizabeth Landon, *The Poor.*)

"Happier he, the peasant, far,
From the pangs of passion free,
That breathes the keen yet wholesome air
of ragged penury."
(Thomas Gray, *Ode on The Pleasure Arising from Vicissitude).*

"*O happy unown'd youths! Your limbs can bear
The scorching dog-star and the winter's air,
While the rich infant, nurs'd with care and pain,
Thirsts with each heat and coughs with every rain.*"
(John Gay. *Trivia.* Bk. II, I. 145.)

"My friends are poor but honest."
(All's Well That Ends Well, I, iii, 201.)

The following illustrate the negative elements in some of the stereotypes of poverty:

"All the days of the poor are evil."
(*Babylonian Talmud,* Kethubot, 110b.)
"He must have a great deal of godliness who can find any satisfaction in being poor."
(Cervantes, *Don Quixote,* Pt. II, Ch. 44.)
"Poverty is no disgrace to a man, but it is confoundedly inconvenient."
(Sydney Smith, *His Wit and Wisdom* (1900), p. 89.)
"The resolutions of a poor man are weak."
(Doolittle, *Chinese Vocabulary* II, 494 (1872.)
"What can a poor man do but love and pray?"
(Hartley Coleridge, *Sonnets—*No. 30)
"If you've really been poor, you remain poor at heart all your life."
(W. Somerset Maugham, Introduction to Arnold Bennett, *The Old Wives Tale,* in *Ten Novels.*)
"The life of the poor is the curse of the heart."
(*Ecclestiasticus,* 38:19.)
"There is no virtue that poverty destroyeth not."
(John Florio. *First Fruits,* Fo. 32.)
"Poverty makes some humble, but more malignant."
(Bulwer-Lytton. *Eugene Aram.* Bk. 1, Ch. 7.)
"The devil wipes his tail with the poor man's pride."
(John Ray. *English Proverbs.* 21.)
"The poor, inur'd to drudgery and distress,
Act without aim, think little, and feel less,
And nowhere, but in feign'd Arcadian scenes,
Taste happiness, or know what pleasure means."
(William Cowper. *Hope* I. 7.)

In short, some see the poor as virtuous, upright, serene, independent, honest, secure, kind, simple and happy, while others see them as evil, mean, violent, sordid and criminal. ⌊ Most people in the United States find it difficult to think of poverty as a stable, persistent, ever present phenomenon, because our expanding economy and the specially favorable circumstances of our history have led to an optimism which makes us think that poverty is transitory. As a matter of fact, the culture of poverty in the United States is indeed of relatively limited scope; but as Michael Harrington and others show, it is probably more widespread than has been generally recognized.⌋

In considering what can be done about the culture of poverty, we must make a sharp distinction between those countries in which it involves a relatively small segment of the population, and those in which it constitutes a very large section. Obviously, the solutions will have to differ in these two areas. In the United States, the major solution proposed by planners and social workers for deal-ing with what are called "multiple problem families," the "undeserving poor," and the "hard core of poverty," is slowly to raise their level of living and eventually incorporate them into the middle class. And, wherever possible, there is some reliance upon psychiatric treatment in an effort to imbue these "shiftless, lazy, unambitious people" with the higher middle-class aspirations.

In the undeveloped countries, where great masses of people share in the culture of poverty, I doubt that social work solutions are feasible. Nor can psychiatrists begin to cope with the magnitude of the problem. They have all they can do to deal with the growing middle class.

In the United States, delinquency, vice and violence represent the major threats to the middle class from the culture of poverty. In our country there is no threat of revolution. In the less developed countries of the world, however, the people who live in the culture of poverty may one day become organized into political movements that seek fundamental revolutionary changes and that is one reason why their existence poses terribly urgent problems.

If my brief outline of the basic psychological aspects of the culture of poverty is essentially sound, then it may be more important to offer the poor of the world's countries a genuinely revolutionary ideology rather than the promise of material goods or a quick rise in the standards of living.

It is conceivable that some countries can eliminate the culture of poverty (at least in the early stages of their industrial revolution) without at first eliminating impoverishment, by changing the value systems and attitudes of the people so they no longer feel helpless and homeless —so they begin to feel that they are living in their own country, with their institutions, their government and their leadership.

November 1963

Life in Appalachia—
the Case of Hugh McCaslin

ROBERT COLES

Hugh McCaslin is unforgettable. He has red hair and, at 43, freckles. He stands six feet four. As he talked to me about his work in the coal mines, I kept wondering what he did with his height down inside the earth.

Once he must have been an unusually powerful man; even today his arms and legs are solid muscle. The fat he has added in recent years has collected in only one place, his waist, both front and back.

I need some padding around my back; it's hurt, and I don't think it'll ever get back right. I broke it bad working, and they told me at first they'd have it fixed in no time flat, but they were wrong. I don't know if they were fooling themselves, or out to fool me in the bargain. It's hard to know *what's* going on around here—that's what I've discovered these last few years.

I'll tell you, a man like me, he has a lot of time to think. He'll sit around here, day upon day, and what else does he have to keep his mind on but his thoughts? I can't

27

work, and even if I could, there's no work to do, not around here, no sir. They told me I'm "totally incapacitated," that's the words they used. They said my spine was hurt, and the nerves, and I can't walk and move about the way I should. As if I needed them to tell me!

Then they gave me exercises and all, and told me I was lucky, because even though I wasn't in shape to go in the mines, I could do anything else, anything that's not too heavy. Sometimes I wonder what goes on in the heads of those doctors. They look you right in the eye, and they're wearing a straight face on, and they tell you you're sick, you've been hurt digging out coal, and you'll never be the same, but you're really not so bad off, because your back isn't so bad you can't be a judge, or a professor, or the president of the coal company or something like that, you know."

Once Hugh McCaslin (not his real name) asked me to look at an X-ray taken of his back and his shoulders—his vertebral column. He persuaded the company doctor to give him the X-ray, or so he said. (His wife told me that he had, in fact, persuaded the doctor's secretary to hand it over, and tell her boss—if he ever asked—that somehow the patient's "file" had been lost.) He was convinced that the doctor was a "company doctor"—which he assuredly was—and a "rotten, dishonest one." Anyway, what did I see in that X-ray? I told him that I saw very little. I am no radiologist, and whatever it was that ailed him could not be dramatically pointed out on an X-ray, or if it could I was not the man to do it. Well, yes he did know that, as a matter of fact:

I got my nerves smashed down there in an accident. I don't know about the bones. I think there was a lot of pressure, huge pressure on the nerves, and it affected the way I walk. The doctor said it wasn't a fracture on a big bone, just one near the spine. He said it wasn't "too serious," that I'd be O.K., just not able to go back to work at least down there.

Then, you see, they closed down the mine itself. That shows you I wasn't very lucky. My friends kept telling me I was lucky to be alive, and lucky to be through with it, being a miner. You know, we don't scare very easy. Together, we never would talk about getting hurt. I suppose it was somewhere in us, the worry; but the first time I heard my friends say anything like that was to me, not to themselves. They'd come by here when I was sick, and they'd tell me I sure was a fortunate guy, and God was smiling that day, and now He'd be smiling forever on me, because I was spared a *real* disaster, and it was bound to come, one day or another. It kind of got me feeling funny, hearing them talk like that *around my bed,* and then seeing them walk off real fast, with nothing to make *them* watch their step and take a pain pill every few hours.

But after a while I thought maybe they did have something; and if I could just recover me a good pension from the company, and get my medical expenses all covered— well, then, I'd get better, as much as possible, and go fetch me a real honest-to-goodness job, where I could see the sun all day, and the sky outside, and breathe our air here, as much of it as I pleased, without a worry in the world.

But that wasn't to be. I was dumb, real dumb, and hopeful. I saw them treating me in the hospital, and when they told me to go home I thought I was better, or soon would be. Instead, I had to get all kinds of treatments, and they said I'd have to pay for them, out of my savings or somewhere. And the pension I thought I was supposed to get, that was all in my mind, they said. They said the coal industry was going through a lot of

changes, and you couldn't expect them to keep people
going indefinitely, even if they weren't in the best of
shape, even if it did happen down in the mines.

Well, that's it, to make it short. I can't do hard work,
and I have a lot of pain, every day of my life. I might be
able to do light work, desk work, but hell, I'm not fit for
anything like that; and even if I could, where's the work
to be found? Around here? Never in a million years.
We're doomed here, to sitting and growing the food we
can and sharing our misery with one another.

My brother, he helps; and my four sisters, they help;
and my daddy, he's still alive and he can't help except to
sympathize, and tell me it's a good thing I didn't get
killed in that landslide and can see my boys grow up.
He'll come over here and we start drinking. You bet, he's
near 80, and we start drinking, and remembering. My
daddy will ask me if I can recollect the time I said I'd
save a thousand dollars for myself by getting a job in the
mines and I say I sure can, and can he recollect the time
he said I'd better not get too greedy, because there's
bad that comes with good in this world, and especially
way down there inside the earth.

He will take a beer or two and then get increasingly
angry. His hair seems to look wilder, perhaps because he
puts his hands through it as he talks. His wife becomes
nervous and tries to give him some bread or crackers, and
he becomes sullen or embarrassingly direct with her. She
is trying to "soak up" his beer. She won't even let it hit his
stomach and stay there a while. She wants it back. He tells
her, "Why don't you *keep* your beer, if you won't let it
do a thing for me?"

They have five sons, all born within nine years. The
oldest is in high school and dreams of the day he will join
the army. He says he will be "taken" in, say, in Charleston
or Beckley—in his mind, any "big city" will do. He will

be sent off to California or Florida or "maybe New York" for basic training; eventually he will "land himself an assignment—anywhere that's good, and it'll be far away from here, I do believe that." Hugh McCaslin becomes enraged when he hears his son talk like that; with a few beers in him he becomes especially enraged:

That's the way it is around here. That's what's happened to us. That's what they did to us. They made us lose any honor we had. They turned us idle. They turned us into a lot of grazing sheep, lucky to find a bit of pasture here and there. We don't *do* anything here anymore; and so my boys, they'll all want to leave, and they will. But they'll want to come back, too—because this land, it's in their bones going way back, and you don't shake off your ancestors that easy, no sir.

My daddy, he was born right up the road in this here hollow, and his daddy, and back to a long time ago. There isn't anyone around here we're not kin to somehow, near or far. My daddy was the one supposed to leave for the mines. He figured he could make more money than he could dream about, and it wasn't too far to go. He went for a while, but some years later he quit. He couldn't take it. I grew up in a camp near the mine, and I'd still be there if it wasn't that I got hurt and moved back here to the hollow. Even while we were at the camp we used to come back here on Sundays, I remember, just like now they come here on weekends from Cincinnati and Dayton and those places, and even from way off in Chicago. I can recall the car we got; everybody talked about it, and when we'd drive as near here as we could—well, the people would come, my grandparents and all my uncles and aunts and cousins, and they'd look and look at that Ford, before they'd see if it was *us,* and say hello to us. I can recollect in my mind being shamed and wanting to disappear in one of those pockets, where my daddy would keep his pipes. My mother would say it wasn't they didn't want to see us, but the Ford, it was real special to them, and could you blame them for not looking at us?

That was when things were really good. Except that even then I don't think we were all that contented. My mother always worried. Every day, come 3 or so in the afternoon, I could tell she was starting to worry. Will anything happen? Will he get hurt? Will they be coming over soon, to give me some bad news? (No, we had no telephone, and neither did the neighbors.) It got so we'd come home from school around 2 or so, and just sit there with her, pretending—pretending to do things, and say things. And then he'd come in, every time. We could hear his voice coming, or his steps, or the door, and we'd all loosen up—and pretend again, that there was nothing we'd worry about, because there wasn't nothing *to* worry about.

One day—I think I was seven or eight, because I was in school, I know that—we had a bad scare. Someone came to the school and told the teacher something, whispered it in her ear. She turned into a sheet, and she looked as though she'd start crying. The older kids knew what had happened, just from her looks. (Yes, it was a one-room schoolhouse, just like the one we have here, only a little bigger.) They ran out, and she almost took off after them, except for the fact that she remembered us. So she turned around and told us there that something bad had happened down in the mines, an explosion, and we should go home and wait there, and if our mothers weren't there—well, wait until they got home.

But we wanted to go with her. Looking back at it, I think she worried us. So she decided to take us, the little ones. And I'll tell you, I can remember that walk with her like it was today. I can see it, and I can tell you what

she said, and what we did, and all. We walked and
walked, and then we came through the woods and there
they were, all of a sudden before our eyes. The people
there, just standing around and almost nothing being
said between them. It was so silent I thought they'd all
turn around and see us, making noise. But, you see, we
must have stopped talking, too, because for a while they
didn't even give us a look over their shoulders. Then we
come closer, and I could hear there was noise after all:
The women were crying, and there'd be a cough or something from some of the miners.

That's what sticks with you, the miners wondering
if their buddies were dead or alive down there. Suddenly
I saw my father, and my mother. They were with their
arms about one another—real unusual—and they were
waiting, like the rest.

Oh, we got home that night, yes, and my daddy said
they were gone—they were dead and we were going
away. And we did. The next week we drove here in our
Ford, and I can hear my daddy saying it wasn't worth
it, money and a car, if you die young, or you live but
your lungs get poisoned, and all that, and you never see
the sun except on Sundays.

But what choice did he have? And what choice did I
have? I thought I might want to do some farming, like
my grandfather, but there's no need for me, and my
grandfather couldn't really keep more than himself
going, I mean with some food and all. Then I thought it'd
be nice to finish school, and maybe get a job someplace
near, in a town not a big city. But everything was
collapsing all over the country then, and you'd be crazy
to think you were going to get anything by leaving here
and going out there, with the lines standing for soup—oh
yes, we heard on the radio what it was like all over.

It could be worse, you say to yourself, and you resolve

to follow your daddy and be a miner. That's what I did. He said we had a lousy day's work, but we got good pay, and we could buy things. My daddy had been the richest man in his family for a while. In fact, he was the only man in his family who had any money at all. After the family looked over our Ford, they'd give us that real tired and sorry look, as though they needed some help real bad, and that's when my daddy would hand out the dollar bills, one after the other. I can picture it right now. You feel rich, and you feel real kind.

Hugh McCaslin's life wouldn't be that much better even if he had not been seriously hurt in a mine accident. The miners who were his closest friends are now unemployed, almost everyone of them. They do not feel cheated out of a disability pension, but for all practical purposes he and they are equally idle, equally bitter, equally sad. With no prompting from my psychiatric mind he once put it this way:

They talk about depressions in this country. I used to hear my daddy talk about them all the time, depressions. It wasn't so bad for my daddy and me in the thirties, when the Big One, the Big Depression, was knocking everyone down, left and right. He had a job, and I knew I was going to have one as soon as I was ready, and I did. Then when the war come, they even kept me home. They said we were keeping everything going over here in West Virginia. You can't run factories without coal. I felt I wouldn't mind going, and getting a look at things out there, but I was just as glad to stay here, I guess. I was married, and we were starting with the kids, so it would have been hard. My young brother, he went. He wasn't yet a miner, and they just took him when he was 18, I think. He come back here and decided to stay out of the mines, but it didn't make much difference in the end, anyway. We're all out of the mines now around here.

So, you see it's *now* that *we're* in a depression. They say things are pretty good in most parts of the country, from what you see on TV, but not so here. We're in the biggest depression ever here: We have no money, and no welfare payments, and we're expected to scrape by like dogs. It gets to your mind after a while. You feel as low as can be, and nervous about everything. That's what a depression does, makes you dead broke, with a lot of bills and the lowest spirits you can ever picture a man having. Sometimes I get up and I'm ready to go over to an undertaker and tell him to do something with me real fast.

I have spent days and nights with the McCaslin family, and Hugh McCaslin doesn't always feel that "low," that depressed, that finished with life. I suppose it can be said that he has "adapted" to the hard, miserable life he faces. At times he shouts and screams about "things," and perhaps in that way keeps himself explicitly angry rather than sullen and brooding. His friends call him a "firebrand," and blame his temper on his red hair. In fact, he says what they are thinking, and need to hear said by someone. They come to see him, and in Mrs. McCaslin's words, "get him going." They bring him homemade liquor to help matters along.

The McCaslins are early risers, but no one gets up earlier than the father. He suffers pain at night; his back and his legs hurt. He has been told that a new hard mattress would help, and hot baths, and aspirin. He spends a good part of the night awake—"thinking and dozing off and then coming to, real sudden-like, with a pain here or there." For a while he thought of sleeping on the floor, or trying to get another bed, but he could not bear the prospect of being alone:

My wife, Margaret, has kept me alive. She has some of God's patience in her, that's the only way I figure she's been able to last it. She smiles when things are so dark you'd think the end has come. She soothes me, and tells me it'll get better, and even though I know it won't I believe her for a few minutes, and that helps.

So he tosses and turns in their bed, and his wife has learned to sleep soundly but to wake up promptly when her husband is in real pain. They have aspirin and treat it as something special—and expensive. I think Hugh McCaslin realizes that he suffers from many different kinds of pain; perhaps if he had more money he might have been addicted to all sorts of pain-killers long ago. Certainly when I worked in a hospital I saw patients like him—hurt and in pain, but not "sick" enough to require hospitalization, and in fact "chronically semi-invalids." On the other hand such patients had tried and failed at any number of jobs. We will never know how Hugh McCaslin might have felt today if he had found suitable work after his accident, or had received further medical care. Work is something a patient needs as he starts getting better, as anyone who works in a "rehabilitation unit" of a hospital well knows. Hugh McCaslin lacked medical care when he needed it, lacks it today, and in his own words needs a "time-killer" as much as a pain-killer. His friends despair, drink, "loaf about," pick up a thing here and there to do, and "waste time real efficiently." So does he—among other things, by dwelling on his injured body.

He dwells on his children, too. There are five of them, and he wants all of them to leave West Virginia. Sometimes in the early morning, before his wife is up, he leaves bed to look at them sleeping:

I need some hope, and they have it, in their young age and the future they have, if they only get the hell out of here before it's too late. Oh, I like it here,too. It's pretty, and all that. It's peaceful. I'm proud of us people. We've been here a long time, and we needed real guts to stay and last. And who wants to live in a big city? I've been in some of our cities, here in West Virginia, and they're no big value, from what I can see, not so far as bringing up a family. You have no land, no privacy, a lot of noise, and all that. But if it's between living and dying, I'll take living; and right here right now, I think we're dying— dying away, slow but sure, every year more and more so.

He worries about his children in front of them. When they get up they see him sitting and drinking coffee in the kitchen. He is wide-awake, and hungrier for company than he knows. He wants to learn what they'll be doing that day. He wants to talk about things, about the day's events and inevitably a longer span of time, the future: "Take each day like your life hangs on it. That's being young, when you can do that, when you're not trapped and have some choice on things." The children are drowsy, but respectful. They go about dressing and taking coffee and doughnuts with him. They are as solicitous as he is. Can they make more coffee? They ask if they can bring him anything— even though they know full well his answer: "No, just yourselves."

Mrs. McCaslin may run the house, but she makes a point of checking every decision with her husband. He "passes on" even small matters—something connected with one of the children's schoolwork, or a neighbor's coming visit, or a project for the church. She is not sly and devious; not clever at appearing weak but "manipulating" all the while. She genuinely defers to her husband, and his weakness, his illness, his inability to find work— and none of those new medical, social, or psychological "developments" have made her see fit to change her ways. Nor is he inclined to sit back and let the world take everything out of his hands. As a matter of fact, it is interesting to see how assertive a man and a father he still is, no matter how awful his fate continues to be. He is *there*, and always there—in spirit as well as in body. I have to compare him

not only with certain Negro fathers I know, who hide from
welfare workers and flee their wives and children in fear
and shame and anger, but also with a wide range of white
middle-class fathers who maintain a round-the-clock
absence from home (for business reasons, for "social"
reasons), or else demonstrate a much-advertised "passivity"
while there. Hugh McCaslin, as poor as one can be in
America, not at all well-educated, jobless, an invalid, and a
worried, troubled man, nevertheless exerts a strong and
continuing influence upon everyone in his family. He is,
again, *there*—not just at home, but very much involved in
almost everything his wife and children do. He talks a lot.
He has strong ideas, and he has a temper. He takes an
interest in all sorts of problems—not only in those that
plague Road's Bend Hollow:

My daddy was a great talker. He wasn't taken in by
the big people who run this county. He didn't read much,
even then when he was young, but he had his beliefs.
He said we don't give everyone a break here, and that's
against the whole purpose of the country, when it was
first settled. You know, there are plenty of people like
him. They know how hard it is for a working man to get
his share—to get *anything*. Let me tell you, if we had a
chance, men like me, we'd vote for a different way of
doing things. It just isn't right to use people like they're
so much dirt, hire them and fire them and give them no
respect and no real security. A few make fortunes and,
the rest of us, we're lucky to have our meals from day to
day. That's not right; it just isn't.

I tell my boys not to be fooled. It's tough out there
in the world, and it's tough here, too. We've got little
here except ourselves. They came in here, the big
companies, and bled us dry. They took everything, our
coal, our land, our trees, our health. We died like we
were in a war, fighting for those companies—and we

were lucky to get enough money to bury our kin. They tell me sometimes I'm bitter, my brothers do, but they're just as bitter as I am—they don't talk as much, that's the only difference. Of course it got better here with unions and with some protection the workers got through the government. But you can't protect a man when the company decides to pull out; when it says it's got all it can get, so goodbye folks, and take care of yourselves, because we're moving on to some other place, and we just can't do much more than tell you it was great while it lasted, and you helped us out a lot, yes sir you did.

He does not always talk like that. He can be quiet for long stretches of time, obviously and moodily quiet. His wife finds his silences hard to bear. She doesn't know what they will "lead to." Every day she asks her husband whether there is anything "special" he wants to eat—even though they both know there isn't much they can afford but the daily mainstays—bread, coffee, doughnuts, crackers, some thin stew, potatoes, homemade jam, biscuits. Mrs. McCaslin defers to her husband, though; one way is to pay him the courtesy of asking him what he wants. I have often heard them go back and forth about food, and as if for all the world they were far better off, with more choices before them:

Anything special you want for supper?

No. Anything suits me fine. I'm not too hungry.

Well, if that's it then I'd better make you hungry with something special.

What can do that?

I thought I'd fry up the potatoes real good tonight and cut in some onions. It's better than boiling, and I've got some good pork to throw in. You wait and see.

I will. It sounds good.

He hurts and she aches for him. His back has its "bad spells," and she claims her own back can "feel the pain that goes through his." They don't touch each other very much in a stranger's presence, or even, I gather, before their children, but they give each other long looks of recognition, sympathy, affection, and sometimes anger or worse. They understand each other in that silent, real, lasting way that defies the gross labels that I and my kind call upon. It is hard to convey in words—theirs or mine—the subtle, delicate, largely unspoken, and continual *sense of each other* (that is the best that I can do) that they have. In a gesture, a glance, a frown, a smile they talk and agree and disagree:

I can tell what the day will be like for Hugh when he first gets up. It's all in how he gets out of bed, slow or with a jump to it. You might say we all have our good days and bad ones, but Hugh has a lot of time to give over to his moods, and around here I guess we're emotional, you might say.

I told her that I thought an outsider like me might not see it that way. She wanted to know what I meant, and I told her: "They call people up in the hollow 'quiet,' and they say they don't show their feelings too much, to each other, let alone in front of someone like me."

Well, I don't know about that, she answered quickly, a bit piqued. I don't know what reasons they have for that. Maybe they don't have good ears. We don't talk *loud* around here, but we say what's on our mind, straightaway, I believe. I never was one for mincing on words, and I'll tell anyone what's on my mind, be he from around here or way over on the other side of the world. I do believe we're cautious here, and we give a man every break we can, because you don't have it easy around here, no matter who you are; so maybe that's why they think we're not given to getting excited and such. But we do.

I went back to Hugh. Did she think he was more

"emotional" than others living nearby?

Well, I'd say it's hard to say. He has a temper, but I think that goes for all his friends. I think he's about ordinary, only because of his sickness he's likely to feel bad more than some, and it comes out in his moods. You know, when we were married he was the most cheerful man I'd ever met. I mean he smiled all the time, not just because someone said something funny. His daddy told me I was getting the happiest of his kids, and I told him I believed he was right, because I'd already seen it for myself. Today he's his old self sometimes, and I almost don't want to see it, because it makes me think back and remember the good times we had.

Oh, we have good times now, too; don't mistake me. They just come rare, compared to when times were good. And always it's his pain that hangs over us; we never know when he'll be feeling right, from day to day.

But when he's got his strength and there's nothing ailing him, he's all set to work, and it gets bad trying to figure what he might do. We talk of moving, but we ask ourselves where we'd go to. We don't want to travel a thousand miles only to be lost in some big city and not have even what we've got. Here there's a neighbor, and our kin, always. We have the house, and we manage to scrape things together, and no one of my kids has ever starved to death. They don't get the food they should, sometimes, but they eat, and they like what I do with food. In fact they complain at church. They say others don't brown the potatoes enough, or the biscuits. and they like a good chocolate cake, and I have that as often as I can.

When Hugh is low-down he doesn't want to get out of bed, but I make him. He'll sit around and not do much. Every few minutes he'll call my name, but then he won't really have much to say. I have those aspirin, but you can't really afford to use them all the time.

When he feels good, though, he'll go do chores. He'll make sure we have plenty of water, and he'll cut away some wood and lay it up nearby. He'll walk up the road and see people. He has friends, you know, who aren't sick like him, but it doesn't do them much good around here to be healthy. They can't work any more than Hugh can. It's bad, all the time bad.

We find our own work, though, and we get paid in the satisfaction you get. We try to keep the house in good shape, and we keep the road clear all year round. That can be a job come winter.

A lot of the time Hugh says he wished he could read better. He'll get an old magazine—the *Reader's Digest*, or the paper from Charleston—and he'll stay with it for hours. I can see he's having a tough time, but it keeps him busy. He tells the kids to remember his mistakes and not to make them all over again. Then they want to know why he made them. And we're off again. He talks about the coal companies and how they bribed us out of our "souls," and how he was a fool, and how it's different now. When they ask what they'll be doing with their reading and writing, it's hard to give them an answer without telling them to move. You don't want to do that, but maybe you do, too. I don't know.

Hugh fought the television. He said it was no good, and we surely didn't have the money to get one. You can get them real cheap, though, secondhand, and there's a chance to learn how to fix it yourself, because some of the men who come back from the army, they've learned how and they'll teach you and do it for you if you ask them. We had to get one, finally. The kids, they said everyone else didn't have the money, any more than we did, but somehow they got the sets, so why couldn't we? That started something, all right. Hugh wanted to know if they thought we could manufacture money. So they wanted to know how the others got their sets. And Hugh said he didn't know, but if they would go find out, and come tell him, why then he'd show them that each family is different, and you can't compare people like that. Well, then they mentioned it to their uncle—he works down there in the school, keeping it in order, and he's on a regular salary, you know, and lives as good as anyone around here, all things told, I'd say. So he came and told us he'd do it, get a set for us, because the kids really need them. They feel left out without TV.

That got Hugh going real bad. He didn't see why the radio wasn't enough, and he wasn't going to take and take and take. He wanted help, but not for a TV set. And then he'd get going on the coal companies, and how we got that radio for cash, and it was brand-new and expensive, but he was making plenty of money then. And he didn't want to go begging, even from kin. And we could just do without, so long as we eat and have a place to sleep and no one's at our door trying to drive us away or take us to jail.

Finally I had to say something. I had to. It was one of the hardest things I've ever had to do. He was getting worse and worse, and the kids they began to think he was wrong in the head over a thing like TV, and they didn't know why; they couldn't figure it out. He said they wouldn't see anything but a lot of trash, and why should we let it all come in here like that? And he said they'd lose interest in school, and become hypnotized or something, and he'd read someplace it happens. And he said gadgets and machines, they came cheap, but you end up losing a lot more than you get, and that was what's happening in America today.

Now, the kids could listen for so long, and they're respectful to him, to both of us, I think you'll agree.

They'd try to answer him, real quiet, and say it wasn't so important, TV wasn't, it was just there to look at, and we would all do it and have a good time. And everyone was having it, but that didn't mean that the world was changing, or that you'd lose anything just because you looked at a picture every once in a while.

And finally, as I say, I joined in. I had to—and I sided with them. I said they weren't going to spend their lives looking at TV, no sir, but it would be okay with me if we had it in the house, that I could live with it, and I think we could all live with it. And Hugh, he just looked at me and didn't say another word, not that day or any other afterwards until much later on, when we had the set already, and he would look at the news and listen real careful to what they tell you might be happening. He told me one day, it was a foolish fight we all had, and television wasn't any better or worse than a lot of other things. But he wished the country would make more than cheap TVs. "We could all live without TV if we had something more to look forward to," he said. I couldn't say anything back. He just wasn't feeling good that day, and to tell the truth TV is good for him when he's like that, regardless of what he says. He watches it like he used to listen to his radio, and he likes it better than he'd ever admit to himself, I'm sure.

On Sundays they go to church. Hugh says he doesn't much believe in "anything," but he goes; he stays home only when he doesn't feel good, not out of any objection to prayer. They all have their Sunday clothes, and they all enjoy getting into them. They become new and different people. They walk together down the hollow and along the road that takes them to a Baptist church. They worship vigorously and sincerely, and with a mixture of awe, bravado, passion, and restraint that leaves an outside observer feeling, well—skeptical, envious, surprised, mystified, admiring, and vaguely nostalgic. I think they emerge much stronger and more united for the experience, and with as much "perspective," I suppose, as others get from different forms of contemplation, submission, and joint participation. Hugh can be as stoic as anyone else, and in church his stoicism can simply pour out. The world *is* confusing, you see. People have *always* suffered, good people. Somewhere, somehow, it is not all for naught—but that doesn't mean one should raise one's hopes too high, not on this earth.

After church there is "socializing," and its importance need not be stressed in our self-conscious age of "groups" that solve "problems" or merely facilitate "interaction." When I have asked myself what "goes on" in those "coffee periods," I remind myself that I heard a lot of people laughing, exchanging news, offering greetings, expressing wishes, fears, congratulations and condolences. I think there is a particular warmth and intensity to some of the meetings because, after all, people do not see much of one another during the week. Yet how many residents of our cities or our suburbs see one another as regularly as these "isolated" people do? Hugh McCaslin put it quite forcefully: We may not see much of anyone for a few days, but Sunday will come and we see everyone we want to see, and by the time we go home we know everything there is to know. As some of us say, they "communicate efficiently.

There is, I think, a certain hunger for companionship that builds up even among people who do not feel as "solitary" as some of their observers have considered them. Particularly at night one feels the woods and the hills close in on "the world." The McCaslins live high up in a hollow, but they don't have a "view." Trees tower over their cabin, and the smoke rising from their chimney has no space at all to dominate. When dusk comes there are no lights to be seen, only their lights to turn on. In winter they eat at about 5 and they are in bed about 7:30 or 8. The last hour before bed is an almost formal time. Every evening Mr. McCaslin smokes his pipe and either reads or carves wood. Mrs. McCaslin has finished putting things away after supper and sits sewing—"mending things and fixing things; there isn't a day goes by that something doesn't tear." The children watch television. They have done what homework they have (or are willing to do) before supper. I have never heard them reprimanded for failing to study. Their parents tell them to go to school; to stay in school; to do well in school—but they aren't exactly sure it makes much difference. They ask the young to study, but I believe it is against their "beliefs" to say one thing and mean another, to children or anyone else.

In a sense, then, they are blunt and truthful with each other. They say what they think, but worry about how to say what they think so that the listener remains a friend or—rather often—a friendly relative. Before going to bed they say good-night, and one can almost feel the reassurance that goes with the greeting. It is very silent "out there" or "outside."

Yes, I think we have good manners, Hugh McCaslin once told me. It's a tradition, I guess, and goes back to Scotland, or so my daddy told me. I tell the kids that they'll know a lot more than I do when they grow up, or I hope they will; but I don't believe they'll have more consideration for people—no sir. We teach them to say hello in the morning, to say good morning, like you said. I know it may not be necessary, but it's good for people living real close to be respectful of one another. And the same goes for the evening.

Now, there'll be fights. You've seen us take after one another. That's okay. But we settle things on the same day, and we try not to carry grudges. How can you carry a grudge when you're just this one family here, and miles away from the next one? Oh, I know it's natural to be spiteful and carry a grudge. But you can only carry it so far, that's what I say. Carry it until the sun goes down, then wipe the slate clean and get ready for another day. I say that a lot to the kids.

Once I went with the McCaslins to a funeral. A great-uncle of Mrs. McCaslin's had died at 72. He happened to be a favorite of hers and of her mother. They lived much nearer to a town than the McCaslins do, and were rather well-to-do. He had worked for the county government all his life—in the Appalachian region, no small position. The body lay at rest in a small church, with hand-picked flowers in bunches around it. A real clan had gathered from all over, as well as friends. Of course it was a sad occasion, despite the man's advanced age; yet even so I was struck by the restraint of the people, their politeness to one another, no matter how close or "near kin" they were. For a moment I watched them move about and tried to block off their subdued talk from my brain. It occurred to me that, were they dressed differently and in a large manor home, they might very much resemble English gentry at a reception. They were courtly people; they looked it and acted it. Many were tall, thin, and close-mouthed. A few were potbellied, as indeed befits a good laugh, but it was always noticeable when it happened. In general they were not exactly demonstrative or talkative, yet they were clearly interested in one another and had very definite and strong sentiments, feelings, emotions, whatever. In other words, as befits the gentry, they had feelings but had them under "appropriate" control. They also seemed suitably resigned, or philosophical—as the circumstances warranted. What crying there was, had already been done. There were no outbursts of any kind, and no joviality either. It was not a wake.

A few days later Hugh McCaslin of Road's Bend Hollow

talked about the funeral and life and death:

He probably went too early, from what I hear. He was in good health, and around here you either die very young—for lack of a doctor—or you really last long. That's the rule, though I admit we have people live to all ages, like anywhere I guess. No, I don't think much of death, even being sick as I am. It happens to you, and you know it, but that's okay. When I was a boy I recall my people burying their old people, right near where we lived. We had a little graveyard, and we used to know all our dead people pretty well. You know, we'd play near their graves, and go ask our mother or daddy about who this one was and what he did, and like that. The other way was through the Bible: Everything was written down on pieces of paper inside the family Bible. There'd be births and marriages and deaths, going way back, I guess as far back as the beginning of the country. I'm not sure of the exact time, but a couple of hundred years, easy.

We don't do that now—it's probably one of the biggest changes, maybe. I mean apart from television and things like that. We're still religious, but we don't keep the records, and we don't bury our dead nearby. It's just not that much of a *home* here, a place that you have and your kin always had and your children and theirs will have, until the end of time, when God calls us all to account. This here place—it's a good house, mind you—but it's just a place I got. A neighbor of my daddy's had it, and he left it, and my daddy heard and I came and fixed it up and we have it for nothing. We worked hard and put a lot into it, and we treasure it, but it never was a *home*, not the kind I knew, and my wife did. We came back to the hollow, but it wasn't like it used to be when we were kids and you felt you were living in the same place all your ancestors did. We're *part* of this land, we were here to start and we'll probably see it die, me or my kids will, the way things are going. There will be no one left here and the stripminers will kill every good acre we have. I thought of that at the funeral. I thought maybe it's just as well to die now, if everything's headed in that direction. I guess that's what happens at a funeral. You get to thinking.

June 1968

FURTHER READING:

Night Comes to the Cumberland by Harry M. Caudill (Boston: Little, Brown & Co., 1963). A first-rate general historical account of the problems that plague Appalachia; probably the best known contemporary work.

Stinking Creek by John Fetterman (New York: E. P. Dutton & Co., 1967). A careful description of one hollow, sensitively done with great candor and honesty.

Yesterday's People by Jack A. Weller (Lexington, Ky., University of Kentucky Press, 1965). A minister's social and cultural observations, along with some accurate, thoughtful, and properly ambiguous conclusions.

Labor Waste in New York:
Rural Exploitation
and Migrant Workers

WILLIAM H. FRIEDLAND

Ever since Congress restricted the importation of Mexican "braceros" into the United States in 1963, farmers have complained about a shortage of seasonal workers to harvest their crops. In fact the number of migrant workers began to decline in the late 1950s. Due in part to mechanization, the decreasing availability of labor created uncertainty among agricultural employers. The removal of more than 150,000 foreign agricultural workers from the labor force in 1964 compounded their anxieties.

While the cutback in foreign labor only indirectly affected East coast agriculture (it had mainly depended on domestic workers), the labor shortage was keenly felt. In New York state, in particular, the number of interstate farm workers has decreased by more than 40 percent since 1955. New York state farmers interviewed during the summer of 1966 uniformly complained about the amount of crops to be harvested and the small numbers of workers coming North. Camps were not filled to capacity. To

salvage the potatoes that ⎯⎯⎯
ground, they finally offered co⎯⎯
in Central New York doubl⎯
migrants.

The farmers attributed the declin⎯
to several factors. They felt that the ⎯
nonagricultural employment in the Un⎯
workers out of agriculture. The cessatio⎯
from Mexico had made East coast migrants ⎯⎯⎯⎯⎯
employers elsewhere and incentives were being ⎯⎯ d to
redirect the labor supply to the Midwest and California.
The farmers also contended that the increased stability in
employment and longer growing season in Florida cut
down the numbers of people who might otherwise move
North.

Troubled by the shortage of migrants, many farmers
believed that mechanization was the solution to their
problems. In some cases, mechanization was out of the
question either because the hardware had not been
developed or because the equipment costs were too high.
In others, the farmers favored mechanization but were
reluctant to employ it since they believed that migrant
crews would bypass their area, leaving the crops that could
not be handled by a machine unharvested.

Though the farmers were convinced that the decline in
the number of migrants was serious, my study of migrant
labor practices in New York State indicates that the
shortage is due more to their inefficient use. Each day time
was wasted because of inadequate scheduling, planning,
and direction. A system which is inefficient and allows for
maximum exploitation and minimum incentive to the
migrant worker was observed.

On New York State farms, labor is still treated as if it
had no intrinsic value; its use is based upon attitudes and
patterns that were developed when labor was plentiful

...p. The following list incorporates some of the ...ns of labor wastage found in migrant camps during the summer of 1966:

Wastage: Poor Scheduling

1. In many crews there is no set time when work begins and considerable time is therefore wasted as crew members are assembled in the morning. The same is true at the end of the day; rumors spread that work is to end shortly and workers stop, only to find that the crew leader expects them to continue. Because there is no fixed time for quitting, the bulk of the crew must wait until a few slower pickers fill out their last unit.

2. Crews are often rushed to the fields only to wait—up to 1 1/2 hours—for the crops to dry.

3. Crews are occasionally assigned to pick a field for the second time when a richer first-pick field is available.

4. A small field that can be completed in a half day is assigned to a crew; under such circumstances, workers often refuse to move to another field.

5. When a move is necessary during the day, long distances between fields frequently discourage workers.

6. In some cases fields have to be prepared before workers can begin picking (e.g., potatoes). Such preparatory work usually is not done in advance and the crew must wait until it is.

Wastage: Poor Planning

1. Where a child-care center is available, it often does not open on time. In such cases, the entire crew must wait until the center opens for the children.

2. Lunch wagons often fail to appear and workers either have to work on empty stomachs or make trips to stores to purchase food.

3. The failure to provide hampers, on occasion, means that little or nothing can be done to increase productivity.

that the crop is stacked on the ground. Workers later have to load the crop in a second (and unpaid) operation.

4. After the field is picked, the crew has to remain until the crop can be weighed. The weighing trucks are often late.

Wastage: Poor Direction

1. Fields are not always easy to find and drivers occasionally lose their way.

2. Crews must wait until the crew leader and the farmer confer over which fields are to be picked.

3. The failure of the farmer to be on hand when the crew appears means that the crew is idle.

4. Confusion in lining workers up in the fields frequently means false starts or other irritations.

5. On completion of the job, the crew occasionally must wait on the bus while the crew leader negotiates payments.

Wastage: Poor Equipment

1. Many busses are unable to start.

2. Busses break down en route to or on return from the fields.

3. Hoes and other tools are not sharp and are not prepared for workers on their arrival.

The burden of labor wastage is placed directly upon the migrant; the time wasted is time he is not paid for. But given the existence of alternative forms of employment today, the old structure of migrant labor with its inherent defects in planning work has created a burden for the farmer as well. Employer attitudes have produced, over the years, a continual deterioration in the work attitudes of the migrants.

Farmers look upon their workers in much the same way that industrial employers did many years ago. Typically, farm employers express beliefs that migrants are lazy and that little or nothing can be done to increase productivity. They frequently contend that "there's no point in paying higher wages, they'll still quit when they've earned $3 for the day." Whether true or not, this attitude toward employees precludes any serious approach to change the situation. Indeed, farmers have developed a whole system of practices that prevent greater efficiency. The prime example of this is the continued dependence of many farmers on the crew leader.

Most farmers prefer to avoid contacts with migrants and leave the control of work to the crew leader. An ex-migrant who becomes a labor contractor by virtue of his ability to purchase or inherit the means of transportation, the crew leader is the primary mediating influence between the workers and the farmer. Because white employers feel that migrants are unpredictable and violent, and because crew members—mostly Negro—view the white world as unpredictable and dangerous, both depend on the crew leader. In a variety of roles, he has enormous power over his crew and their productivity.

An owner of transportation, usually school busses and trucks, the crew leader is also an entrepreneur in the sense that he risks his capital in contracts with employers and in recruiting workers. Once he arrives North, the crew leader's role changes to that of camp manager. Responsible for the direction and maintenance of his crew within the camp, he provides food, alcohol, and auxiliary services including transportation. He maintains law and order in the camp, transports labor to the work site and, at the field, acts as job foreman allocating specific tasks to workers, managing all aspects of the operation until the produce is actually delivered to the packing houses. In addition, the crew leader serves as a banker to his crew, lending them money either directly or through credit for food, alcohol or transportation.

The crew leader can sometimes earn as much money, if not more, from these peripheral roles than he can from the output of his crew. Indeed, when the farmer abdicates control of work organization to the crew leader, he yields it to a person whose interests in productivity have little relation to his. But though the crew leader has many talents, he is in most cases unable to cope with the problems of effectively managing workers.

The maintenance of control within the camp and the work place, for example, is one crucial responsibility that the crew leader honors more in the breach than in reality. Theoretically, his role as "provider" gives him the leverage to control the output of his crew, to ensure that workers turn out for work every day and that they work steadily and regularly in the fields. The crew leader, however, has little experience preparing him to deal directly with problems of efficiency let alone the power to make decisions and plans crucial to determining the organization of work. More than half of the examples of wastage cited above are beyond his control, developed in part from the lack of communication between employer and those working for him.

The effects of labor wastage upon the migrant are clear. In none of the examples cited are migrants paid for time lost. The migrant can only conclude, and does, that his time has no value. Prey to the other exploitative structures (the high cost of credit, food, and alcohol) and other debilitating experiences (the lack of control within the camps, the unpredictability of life, and the nonexistence of savings structures), the migrant has little incentive to work more effectively or to accumulate income. The daily loss of time, frequently amounting to 25 percent of work time, cannot possibly be conducive to productivity. If it is made continually clear to a person that his time is of no value, it can hardly be expected that he will hurry to get on the bus in the morning or utilize his time well while in the fields.

No attempt is being made here to argue that migrants have a "Protestant Ethic" toward work which is drained from them by the present structure. In all employment situations, there are many types of attitudes toward work: attitudes that support working hard and others that do not. But in all employment relationships it is necessary to create structures which maximize the productivity of all employees. Although many migrants come North with the intention of earning more than a subsistence wage, productivity even among the best workers is low. Their intentions are rapidly squelched by two aspects of the present structure of migrant labor.

First the system of employee recruitment is inadequate and imposes serious economic hardships on the migrant. Because of the ostensible shortage of workers, farmers all too frequently hoard labor by getting their crews on hand early or by keeping them between an early and a late season. Thus, already in debt to the crew leader who usually supports him en route, the migrant arrives in camp only to find that work will be sparse for some time. During this period, his debt to the crew leader who supplies food on credit, increases. By the time the season starts, the worker's expectations have been realistically set at simply maintaining himself.

Asked how much money they expected to take back South, one migrant summed up most attitudes saying: "I'll break even; I came with nothing and I'll leave with nothing." Some replied that they might make $30 or "$100-$200 if I'm lucky." The northern trip is now viewed as necessary to "get through" the year while work in the South is seen as a time when some money is made. Based on the low wage levels and irregularity of work in New York state, these attitudes create the "$3-a-day" syndrome with which farmers justify their low wages.

Second, low productivity is related to the day-to-day organization of work in the fields. Sending a crew to a field which has had a first picking or to a small field which can be finished in less than a day, or where, for whatever reason, the picking is poor, is feasible only when there is a surplus of labor. Not only is the work slower and more tiring in such fields but a change of fields during the day entails a loss of time in transport. Workers become discouraged and refuse to continue to work.

Until closer planning and scheduling are introduced, the present organization of work cannot yield higher outputs by migrants. Discouraged by the conditions, migrants have developed four responses:

1. Griping. "They have no business bringing people to a field like this." "I'll never come North again; it's not worth it."

2. The walk-off. If the field is considered poor, migrants will leave saying, "It doesn't pay to kill yourself for things like this."

3. "Target" working. "I'll just get enough to buy my dinner and a bottle and I'll quit."

4. The slow-down. This most common response occurs particularly when workers are paid by the hour but is also found on piecework jobs. The technique is old and well-established: one looks busy by standing or squatting in a working position without doing much work. If one works harder than the others, on hourly work, sanctions are strong and immediate: "Don't take us out of a job."

Even for the productive individual, the organization of work is a discouraging one. Movements of the crew, poor fields, poor planning and scheduling, and breakdowns of equipment mean that he can rarely earn $10 a day *even if he is prepared to work extremely hard.* Exploitation by the crew leader and the difficulty of saving money all add up to few built-in incentives that can support the productive worker. He soon takes on the attitudes of the prevalent migrant culture or drops out of the migrant labor stream. In 1952, Arthur M. Ross and Samuel Liss prepared a report for a Senate hearing on migrant labor saying:

> . . . the contractor system is a highly effective device for transferring the risk of agricultural employment to the workers. It is a sound principle of industrial relations that the various economic risks incident to employment ought to be distributed fairly or else insured against. This principle is notably absent in agricultural harvest work. Anyone familiar with urban industrial relations would suppose, for example, that employers would have some responsibility for workers who are brought to a work situation and held there for several weeks although no work is furnished to them. In agriculture, however, it frequently happens that the workers are brought into a grower's camp, upon specific instruction from the grower, several weeks before they are needed, and remain entirely on their own until work begins, unless public charity is available or the contractor is willing to give advances of money or of credit. The situation is the same whether the lack of work is due to the vagaries of weather, the conditions of the market, miscalcualtion on the part of the grower, or any other reason. . . . Whatever the source of risk, it is borne by the individuals who are least able to undertake it.

Seventeen years later little has changed despite the fact that Public Law 414 adopted in 1963 requires the registration of labor contractors and the exclusion of non-Americans from seasonal work. The system remains much as Ross and Liss described it and the migrant workers themselves— those least able to undertake the cost of the risks of harvest —continue to sustain most of its costs because of an outmoded system of production.

But the adoption of Public Law 414 has created the base for a serious change in agriculture. The shortage of labor it imposes by its restrictions on braceros, can induce farmers to change the organization of work and control of labor. Pressure to develop techniques for effective manpower direction can be applied by farmers on the agricultural colleges, research stations and extension services that have made American agriculture the powerful force it is today. Yet as long as farmers continue to look to "hardware" as the only solution to their problems, labor will continue to be managed by mechanization, by getting rid of it.

The long experience of industry will have to be brought to bear on the managerial problem. Farmers will have to internalize the idea that labor has intrinsic cash value and that its efficient organization is crucial to the farmers' own welfare. The incentives which must be brought to a new organization of work not only have to do with better wages but with better planning, organizing, scheduling, and controlling. When those people interested in more than minimal survival learn that they can earn money, the trip North will again become attractive to better workers.

Any conclusions with respect to policy must be formulated in the most tentative way since the research reported here is preliminary and much additional work remains to be done. The experience of field work, however, indicates that careful planning of an even rudimentary nature can eliminate some of forms of wastage noted. Individual farmers, for example, can provide crew leaders and their bus drivers with maps that get them to the fields without getting lost. Scheduling of work can take place more effectively. Farmers can exercise greater control over order in their camps rather than abdicating their responsibility. Savings systems can be created to encourage better workers to accumulate money. Or farmers can insist that pricing of food provided by the crew leader be less exploitative.

While these and many other changes are possible, the likelihood remains that mechanisms that ensure greater equality in the sharing of economic risks will be required if a significant proportion of the migrant population is to be effected. The experience of urban industry has shown that only when the employer bears the financial costs of inefficiency does he become significantly motivated to insure more effective management.

Legislation requiring door-to-door wages (from the South), the guarantee of an eight-hour day after arrival in the North and/or the guarantee of a fixed number of days of work are just some ways the risks of harvest can be redistributed. Until the cash value of labor is made explicit to agricultural employers through external pressure, few changes in farmer attitudes will be forthcoming. Legislation that throws the burden of risk upon farmers would produce an immediate reaction from the research agencies associated with agriculture who would begin to provide techniques of more effective management almost immediately. The consequences for efficiency in agriculture and living standards for migrant workers would be enormous.
February 1969

FURTHER READING:

Men on the Move by Nels Anderson (Chicago: University of Chicago Press, 1940). Although outdated, this is a definitive sociological work on agricultural workers.

The Slaves We Rent by Truman Moore (New York: Random House, 1965) is a first-class journalistic account of the situation of migrant workers throughout the country.

The Ground Is Our Table by Steve Allen (New York: Doubleday, 1966). Written in anger from his personal experiences with poverty, this book focuses on agricultural labor in the Southwest and includes an enthusiastic endorsement of the Chavez organization.

Farmers, Workers and Machines: Technological and Social Change in Farm Industries of Arizona by Harland Padfield and William E. Martin (Tucson: University of Arizona Press, 1965). This book contains economic data on various crops and also empirical data on agricultural workers in Arizona with special emphasis on differences in ethnic groups.

The Serpent-Handling
Religions of West Virginia

NATHAN L. GERRARD

". . . And these signs shall follow them that believe; In my name shall they cast out devils; they shall speak with new tongues; They shall take up serpents; and if they drink any deadly thing, it shall not hurt them; they shall lay hands on the sick, and they shall recover." *Mark* 16:17-18

In Southern Appalachia, two dozen or three dozen fundamentalist congregations take this passage literally and "take up serpents." They use copperheads, water moccasins, and rattlesnakes in their religious services.

The serpent-handling ritual was inaugurated between 1900 and 1910, probably by George Went Hensley. Hensley began evangelizing in rural Grasshopper Valley, Tennessee, then traveled widely throughout the South, particularly in Kentucky, spreading his religion. He died in Florida at 70—of snakebite. To date, the press has reported about 20 such deaths among the serpent-handlers. One other death was recorded last year, in Kentucky.

For seven years, my wife and I have been studying a number of West Virginia serpent-handlers, primarily in order to discover what effect this unusual form of religious practice has on their lives. Although serpent-handling is outlawed by the state legislatures of Kentucky, Virginia, and Tennessee and by municipal ordinances in North Carolina, it is still legal in West Virginia. One center is the Scrabble Creek Church of All Nations in Fayette County, about 37 miles from Charleston. Another center is the Church of Jesus in Jolo, McDowell County, one of the most poverty-stricken areas of the state. Serpent-handling is also practiced sporadically elsewhere in West Virginia, where it is usually led by visitors from Scrabble Creek or Jolo.

The Jolo church attracts people from both Virginia and Kentucky, in addition to those from West Virginia. Members of the Scrabble Creek church speak with awe of the Jolo services, where people pick up large handfuls of posisonous snakes, fling them to the ground, pick them up again, and thrust them under their shirts or blouses, dancing ecstatically. We attended one church service in Scrabble Creek where visitors from Jolo covered their heads with clusters of snakes and wore them as crowns.

Serpent-handling was introduced to Scrabble Creek in 1941 by a coal miner from Harlan, Kentucky. The practice really began to take hold in 1946, when the present leader of the Scrabble Creek church, then a member of the Church of God, first took up serpents. The four or five original serpent-handlers in Fayette County met at one another's homes until given the use of an abandoned one-room school house in Big Creek. In 1959, when their number had swelled several times over, they moved to a larger church in Scrabble Creek.

During the course of our seven-year study, about a dozen members of the church received snakebites. (My wife and

I were present on two of these occasions.) Although there were no deaths, each incident was widely and unfavorably publicized in the area. For their part, the serpent-handlers say the Lord causes a snake to strike in order to refute scoffers' claims that the snakes' fangs have been pulled. They see each recovery from snakebite as a miracle wrought by the Lord—and each death as a sign that the Lord "really had to show the scoffers how dangerous it is to obey His commandments." Since adherents believe that death brings one to the throne of God, some express an eagerness to die when He decides they are ready. Those who have been bitten and who have recovered seem to receive special deference from other members of the church.

The ritual of serpent-handling takes only 15 or 20 minutes in religious sessions that are seldom shorter than four hours. The rest of the service includes singing Christian hymns, ecstatic dancing, testifying, extemporaneous and impassioned sermons, faith-healing, "speaking in tongues," and foot-washing. These latter ritials are a part of the firmly-rooted Holiness movement, which encompasses thousands of churches in the Southern Appalachian region. The Holiness churches started in the nineteenth century as part of a perfectionist movement.

The social and psychological functions served by the Scrabble Creek church are probably very much the same as those served by the more conventional Holiness churches. Thus, the extreme danger of the Scrabble Creek rituals probably helps to validate the members' claims to holiness. After all, the claim that one is a living saint is pretentious even in a sacred society—and it is particularly difficult to maintain in a secular society. That the serpent-handler regularly risks his life for his religion is seen as evidence of his saintliness. As the serpent-handler stresses over and over, "I'm afraid of snakes like anybody else, but when God anoints me, I handle them with joy." The fact that he is usually not bitten, or if bitten usually recovers, is cited as further evidence of his claim to holiness.

After we had observed the Scrabble Creek serpent-handlers for some time, we decided to give them psychological tests. We enlisted the aid of Auke Tellegen, department of psychology, University of Minnesota, and three of his clinical associates: James Butcher, William Schofield, and Anne Wirt. They interpreted the Minnesota Multiphasic Personality Inventory that we administered to 50 serpent-handlers (46 were completed)—and also to 90 members of a conventional denomination church 20 miles from Scrabble Creek. What we wanted to find out was how these two groups differed.

What we found were important personality differences not only between the serpent-handlers and the conventional church members, but also between the older and the younger generations within the conventional group. We believe that these differences are due, ultimately, to differences in social class: The serpent-handlers come from the nonmobile working class (average annual income: $3000), whereas members of the conventional church are upwardly mobile working-class people (average annual income: $5000) with their eyes on the future.

But first, let us consider the similarities between the two groups. Most of the people who live in the south central part of West Virginia, serpent-handlers or not, have similar backgrounds. The area is rural, nonfarm, with only about one-tenth of the population living in settlements of more than 2500. Until recently, the dominant industry was coal-mining, but in the last 15 years mining operations have been drastically curtailed. The result has been widespread unemployment. Scrabble Creek is in that part of Appalachia that has been officially declared a "depressed area"—which means that current unemployment rates there often equal those of the depression.

There are few foreign-born in this part of West Virginia. Most of the residents are of Scottish-Irish or Pennsylvania Dutch descent, and their ancestors came to the New World so long ago that there are no memories of an Old World past.

Generally, public schools in the area are below national standards. Few people over 50 have had more than six or seven years of elementary education.

Religion has always been important here. One or two generations ago, the immediate ancestors of both serpent-handlers and conventional-church members lived in the same mining communities and followed roughly the same religious practices. Today there is much "backsliding," and the majority seldom attend church regularly. But there is still a great deal of talk about religion, and there are few professed atheists.

Though the people of both churches are native-born Protestants with fundamentalist religious beliefs, little education, and precarious employment, the two groups seem to handle their common problems in very different ways. One of the first differences we noticed was in the way the older members of both churches responded to illness and old age. Because the members of both churches had been impoverished and medically neglected during childhood and young adulthood, and because they had earned their livelihoods in hazardous and health-destroying ways, they were old before their time. They suffered from a wide variety of physical ailments. Yet while the older members of the conventional church seemed to dwell morbidly on their physical disabilities, the aged serpent-handlers seemed able to cheerfully ignore their ailments.

The serpent-handlers, in fact, went to the opposite extreme. Far from being pessimistic hypochondriacs like the conventional-church members, the serpent-handlers were so intent on placing their fate in God's benevolent hands that they usually failed to take even the normal precautions in caring for their health. Three old serpent-handlers we knew in Scrabble Creek were suffering from serious cardiac conditions. But when the Holy Spirit moved them, they danced ecstatically and violently. And they did this without any apparent harm.

No matter how ill the old serpent-handlers are, unless they are actually prostrate in their beds they manage to attend and enjoy church services lasting four to six hours, two or three times a week. Some have to travel long distances over the mountains to get to church. When the long sessions are over, they appear refreshed rather than weary.

One evening an elderly woman was carried into the serpent-handling church in a wheelchair. She had had a severe stroke and was almost completely paralyzed. Wheeled to the front of the church, she watched everything throughout the long services. During one particularly frenzied singing and dancing session, the fingers of her right hand tapped lightly against the arm of the chair. This was the only movement she was able to make, but obviously she was enjoying the service. When friends leaned over and offered to take her home, she made it clear she was not ready to go. She stayed until the end, and gave the impression of smiling when she was finally wheeled out. Others in the church apparently felt pleased rather than depressed by her presence.

Both old members of the conventional denomination and old serpent-handlers undoubtedly are frequently visited by the thought of death. Both rely on religion for solace, but the serpent-handlers evidently are more successful. The old serpent-handlers are not frightened by the prospect of death. This is true not only of those members of the minority who do not handle serpents.

One 80-year-old member of the Scrabble Creek church—

who did not handle serpents—testified in our presence: "I am not afraid to meet my Maker in Heaven. I am ready. If somebody was to wave a gun in my face, I would not turn away. I am in God's hands."

Another old church member, a serpent-handler, was dying from silicosis. When we visited him in the hospital he appeared serene, although he must have known that he would not live out the week.

The assertion of some modern theologians that whatever meaning and relevance God once may have had has been lost for modern man does not apply to the old serpent-handlers. To them, God is real. In fact, they often see Him during vivid hallucinations. He watches over the faithful. Misfortune and even death do not shake their faith, for misfortune is interpreted, in accordance with God's inscrutable will, as a hidden good.

Surprisingly, the contrast between the optimistic old serpent-handlers and the pessimistic elders of the conventional church all but disappeared when we shifted to the younger members of the two groups. Both groups of young people, on the psychological tests, came out as remarkably well adjusted. They showed none of the neurotic and depressive tendencies of the older conventional-church members. And this cheerful attitude prevailed despite the fact that many of them, at least among the young serpent-handlers, had much to be depressed about.

The young members of the conventional church are much better off, socially and economically, than the young serpent-handlers. The parents of the young conventional-church members can usually provide the luxuries that most young Americans regard as necessities. Many conventional-church youths are active in extracurricular activities in high school or are attending college. The young serpent-handlers, in contrast, are shunned and stigmatized as "snakes." Most young members of the conventional denomination who are in high school intend to go on to college, and they will undoubtedly attain a higher socio-economic status than their parents have attained. But most of the young serpent-handlers are not attending school. Many are unemployed. None attend or plan to attend college, and they often appear quite depressed about their economic prospects.

The young serpent-handlers spend a great deal of time wandering aimlessly up and down the roads of the hollows, and undoubtedly are bored when not attending church. Their conversation is sometimes marked by humor, with undertones of synicism and bitterness. We are convinced that what prevents many of them from becoming delinquent or demoralized is their wholehearted participation in religious practices that provide an acceptable outlet for their excess energy, and strengthen their self-esteem by giving them the opportunity to achieve "holiness."

Now, how does all this relate to the class differences between the serpent-handlers and the conventional church group? The answer is that what allows the serpent-handlers to cope so well with their problems—what allows the older members to rise above the worries of illness and approaching death, and the younger members to remain relatively well-adjusted despite their grim economic prospects—is a certain approach to life that is typical of them as members of the stationary working class. The key to this approach is hedonism.

The psychological tests showed that the young serpent-handlers, like their elders, were more impulsive and spontaneous than the members of the conventional church. This may account for the strong appeal of the Holiness churches to those members of the stationary working class who prefer religious hedonism to reckless hedonism, with its high incidence of drunkenness and illegitimacy. Religious hedonism is compatible with a puritan morality—and it compensates for its constraints.

The feeling that one cannot plan for the future, expressed in religious terms as "being in God's hands," fosters the widespread conviction among members of the stationary working class that opportunities for pleasure must be exploited immediately. After all, they may never occur again. This attitude is markedly different from that of the upwardly mobile working class, whose members are willingto postpone immediate pleasures for the sake of long-term goals.

Hedonism in the stationary working class is fostered in childhood by parental practices that, while demanding obedience in the home, permit the child license outside the home. Later, during adulthood, this orientation toward enjoying the present and ignoring the future is reinforced by irregular employment and the other insecurities of stationary working-class life. In terms of middle-class values, hedonism is self-defeating. But from a psychiatric point of view, for those who actually have little control of their position in the social and economic structure of modern society, it may very well aid acceptance of the situation. This is particularly true when it takes a religious form of expression. Certainly, hedonism and the associated trait of spontaneity seen in the old serpent-handlers form a very appropriate attitude toward life among old people who can no longer plan for the future.

In addition to being more hedonistic than members of the conventional church, the serpent-handlers are also more exhibitionistic. This exhibitionism and the related need for self-revelation are, of course, directly related to the religious practices of the serpent-handling church. But frankness, both about others and themselves, is typical of stationary working-class people in general. To a large extent, this explains the appeal of the Holiness churches. Ordinarily, their members have little to lose from frankness, since their status pretensions are less than those of the upwardly mobile working class, who are continually trying to present favorable images of themselves.

Because the young members of the conventional denomination are upwardly mobile, they tend to regard their elders as "old-fashioned," "stick-in-the-muds," and "ignorant." Naturally, this lack of respect from their children and grandchildren further depresses the sagging morale of the older conventional-church members. They respond resentfully to the tendency of the young "to think they know more than their elders." The result is a vicious circle of increasing alienation and depression among the older members of the conventional denomination.

There appears to be much less psychological incompatibility between the old and the young serpent-handlers. This is partly because the old serpent-handlers manage to retain a youthful spontaneity in their approach to life. Then too, the young serpent-handlers do not take a superior attitude toward their elders. They admire their elders for their greater knowledge of the Bible, which both old and young accept as literally true. And they also admire their elders for their handling of serpents. The younger church members, who handle snakes much less often than the older members do, are much more likely to confess an ordinary, everday fear of snakes—a fear that persists until overcome by strong religious emotion.

Furthermore, the young serpent-handlers do not expect to achieve higher socioeconomic status than their elders. In fact, several young men said they would be satisfied if they could accomplish as much. From the point of view of the stationary working class, many of the older serpent-handlers are quite well-off. They sometimes draw two pensions, one from the Social Security and one from the United Mine Workers.

Religious serpent-handling, then—and all the other

emotionalism of the Holiness churches that goes with it
—serves a definite function in the lives of its adherents.
It is a safety valve for many of the frustrations of life in
present-day Appalachia. For the old, the serpent-handling
religion helps soften the inevitability of poor health, illness,
and death. For the young, with their poor educations and
poor hopes of finding sound jobs, its promise of holiness
is one of the few meaningful goals in a future dominated
by the apparent inevitability of lifelong poverty and
idleness.
May 1968

FURTHER READING:

They Shall Take Up Serpents by Weston Labarre (Minneapolis: University of Minnesota Press, 1962). A psychological interpretation of serpent-handling and its history.

"Ordeal by Serpents, Fire and Strychnine" by Berthold Schwarz, *Psychiatric Quarterly*, 1960, 405-429. The author personally observed more than 200 instances of serpent-handling.

The Small Sects in America by Elmert T. Clark (New York: Abingdon Press, 1959). An excellent account of the holiness movement, of which the serpent-handling sect is an offshoot.

Life and Religion in Southern Appalachia by W. D. Weatherford and Earl D. C. Brewer (New York: Friendship Press, 1962). The role of religion in the life of the rural poor in Appalachia.

White Gangs

WALTER B. MILLER

If one thinks about street corner gangs at all these days, it is probably in the roseate glow of *West Side Story*, itself the last flowering of a literary and journalistic concern that goes back at least to the late 1940s. Those were the days when it seemed that the streets of every city in the country had become dark battlefields where small armies of young men engaged their honor in terrible trials of combat, clashing fiercely and suddenly, then retiring to the warm succor of their girl cohorts. The forward to a 1958 collection of short stories, *The Young Punks*, captures a bit of the flavor:

These are the stories behind today's terrifying headlines—about a strange new frightening cult that has grown up in our midst. Every writer whose work is included in this book tells the truth. These kids are tough. Here are knife-carrying killers, and thirteen-year-old street walkers who could give the most hardened call-girl lessons. These kids pride themselves on their "ethics": never go chicken, even if it means knifing your own friend in the back. Never rat on a guy who wears your gang colors, unless he rats on you first. Old men on crutches are fair game. If a chick plays you for a sucker, blacken her eyes and walk away fast.

Today, the one-time devotee of this sort of stuff might be excused for wondering where they went, the Amboy Dukes and all those other adolescent warriors and lovers who so excited his fancy a decade ago. The answer, as we shall see, is quite simple—nowhere. The street gangs are still there, out on the corner where they always were.

The fact is that the urban adolescent street gang is as old as the American city. Henry Adams, in his *Education*, describes in vivid detail the gang fights between the North-siders and Southsiders on Boston Common in the 1840s. An observer in 1856 Brooklyn writes: ". . . at any and all hours there are multitudes of boys . . . congregated on the corners of the streets, idle in their habits, dissolute in their conduct, profane and obscene in their conversation, gross and vulgar in their manners. If a female passes one of the groups she is shocked by what she sees and hears. . . ." The Red Raiders of Boston have hung out on the same corner at least since the 1930s; similarly, gang fighting between the Tops and Bottoms in West Philadelphia, which started in the thirties is still continuing in 1969.

Despite this historical continuity, each new generation tends to perceive the street gang as a new phenomenon generated by particular contemporary conditions and destined to vanish as these conditions vanish. Gangs in the 1910s and 1920s were attributed to the cultural dislocations and community disorganization accompanying the mass immigration of foreigners; in the thirties to the enforced idleness and economic pressures produced by the Great Depression; in the fifties to the emotional disturbance of parents and children caused by the increased stresses and tensions of modern life. At present, the existence of gangs is widely attributed to a range of social injustices: racial discrimination, unequal educational and work opportunities, resentment over inequalities in the distribution of wealth and privilege in an affluent society, and the ineffective or oppressive policies of service agencies such as the police and the schools.

There is also a fairly substantial school of thought that holds that the street gangs are disappearing or have already disappeared. In New York City, the stage of so many real and fictional gang dramas of the fifties and early sixties, the *Times* sounded their death-knell as long ago as 1966. Very often, the passing of the gang is explained by the notion that young people in the slums have converted their gang-forming propensities into various substitute activities. They have been knocked out by narcotics, or they have been "politicized" in ways that consume their energies in radical or reform movements, or their members have become involved in "constructive" commercial activities, or enrolled in publicly financed education and/or work-training programs.

As has often been the case, these explanations are usually based on very shaky factual grounds and derived from rather parochial, not to say self-serving, perspectives. For street gangs are not only still widespread in United States cities, but some of them appear to have again taken up "gang warfare" on a scale that is equal to or greater than the phenomenon that received so much attention from the media in the 1950s.

In Chicago, street gangs operating in the classic formations of that city—War Lords, High Supremes, Cobra Stones—accounted for 33 killings and 252 injuries during the first six months of 1969. Philadelphia has experienced a wave of gang violence that has probably resulted in more murders in a shorter period of time than during any equivalent phase of the "fighting gang" era in New York. Police estimate that about 80 gangs comprising about 5,000 members are "active" in the city, and that about 20 are engaged in combat. Social agencies put the total estimated number of gangs at 200, with about 80 in the "most hostile" category. Between October 1962 and December 1968, gang members were reportedly involved in 257 shootings, 250 stabbings and 205 "rumbles." In the period between January 1968 and June 1969, 54 homicides and over 520 injuries were attributed to armed battles between gangs. Of the murder victims, all but eight were known to be affiliated with street gangs. The assailants ranged in age from 13 to 20, with 70 percent of them between 16 and 18 years old. Most of these gangs are designated by the name of the major corner where they hang out, the 12th and Poplar Streeters, or the 21 W's (for 21st and Westmoreland). Others bear traditional names such as the Centaurs, Morroccos and Pagans.

Gangs also continue to be active in Boston. In a single 90-minute period on May 10, 1969, one of the two channels of the Boston Police radio reported 38 incidents involving gangs, or one every 2 1/2 minutes. This included two gang fights. Simultaneous field observation in several white lower-class neighborhoods turned up evidence that gangs were congregating at numerous street corners throughout the area.

Although most of these gangs are similar to the classic types to be described in what follows, as of this summer the national press had virtually ignored the revival of gang violence. *Time* magazine did include a brief mention of "casual mayhem" in its June 27 issue, but none of the 38 incidents in Boston on May 10 was reported even in the local papers. It seems most likely, however, that if all this had been going on in New York City, where most of the media have their headquarters, a spate of newspaper features, magazine articles and television "specials" would have created the impression that the country was being engulfed by a "new" wave of gang warfare. Instead, most people seem to persist in the belief that the gangs have disappeared or that they have been radically transformed.

This anomalous situation is partly a consequence of the problem of defining what a gang is (and we will offer a definition at the end of our discussion of two specific gangs), but it is also testimony to the fact that this enduring aspect of the lives of urban slum youth remains complex and poorly understood. It is hoped that the following examination of the Bandits and the Outlaws—both of Midcity— will clarify at least some of the many open questions about street corner gangs in American cities.

Midcity, which was the location of our 10-year gang study project (1954-64), is not really a city at all, but a portion of a large one, here called Port City. Midcity is a predominantly lower-class community with a relatively high rate of crime, in which both criminal behavior and a characteristic set of conditions—low-skill occupations, little education, low-rent dwellings, and many others— appeared as relatively stable and persisting features of a developed way of life. How did street gangs fit into this picture?

In common with most major cities during this period, there were many gangs in Midcity, but they varied widely in size, sex composition, stability and range of activities. There were about 50 Midcity street corners that served as hangouts for local adolescents. Fifteen of these were "major" corners, in that they were rallying points for the full range of a gang's membership, while the remaining 35 were "minor," meaning that in general fewer groups of smaller size habitually hung out there.

In all, for Midcity in this period, 3,650 out of 5,740, or 64 percent, of Midcity boys habitually hung out at a particular corner and could therefore be considered members of a particular gang. For girls, the figure is 1,125 out of 6,250, or 18 percent. These estimates also suggest that something like 35 percent of Midcity's boys, and 80 percent of its girls, did *not* hang out. What can be said about them? What made them different from the approximately 65 percent of the boys and 20 percent of the girls who did hang out?

Indirect evidence appears to show that the practice of hanging out with a gang was more prevalent among lower-status adolescents, and that many of those who were not known to hang out lived in middle-class or lower-class I (the higher range of the lower-class) areas. At the same time, however, it is evident that a fair proportion of higher-status youngsters also hung out. The question of status, and its relation to gang membership and gang behavior is very complex, but it should be borne in mind as we now take a closer look at the gangs we studied.

The Bandit Neighborhood

Between the Civil War and World War II, the Bandit neighborhood was well-known throughout the city as a colorful and close-knit community of Irish laborers. Moving to a flat in one of its ubiquitous three-decker frame tenements represented an important step up for the impoverished potato-famine immigrants who had initially settled in the crowded slums of central Port City. By the 1810s the second generation of Irish settlers had produced a spirited and energetic group of athletes and politicos, some of whom achieved national prominence.

Those residents of the Bandit neighborhood who shared in some degree the drive, vitality and capability of these famous men assumed steady and fairly remunerative positions in the political, legal and civil service world of Port City, and left the neighborhood for residential areas whose green lawns and single houses represented for them what Midcity had represented for their fathers and grandfathers. Those who lacked these qualities remained in the Bandit neighborhood, and at the outset of World War II made up a stable and relatively homogeneous community of low-skilled Irish laborers.

The Bandit neighborhood was directly adjacent to Midcity's major shopping district, and was spotted with bars, poolrooms and dance halls that served as meeting places for an active neighborhood social life. Within two blocks of the Bandits' hanging-out corner were the Old Erin and New Hibernia dance halls, and numerous drinking establishments bearing names such as the Shamrock, Murphy and Donoghue's and the Emerald Bar and Grill.

A number of developments following World War II disrupted the physical and social shape of the Bandit community. A mammoth federally-financed housing project sliced through and blocked off the existing network of streets and razed the regular rows of wooden tenements. The neighborhood's small manufacturing plants were progressively diminished by the growth of a few large establishments, and by the 1950s the physical face of the neighborhood was dominated by three large and growing plants. As these plants expanded they bought off many of the properties which had not been taken by the housing project, demolished buildings, and converted them into acres of black-topped parking lots for their employees.

During this period, the parents of the Bandit corner gang members stubbornly held on to the decreasing number of low-rent, deteriorating, private dwelling units. Although the Bandits' major hanging corner was almost surrounded by the housing project, virtually none of the gang members lived there. For these families, residence in the housing project would have entailed a degree of financial stability and restrained behavior that they were unable or unwilling to assume, for the corner gang members of the Bandit neighborhood were the scions of men and women who occupied the lowest social level in Midcity. For them low rent was a passion, freedom to drink and to behave drunkenly a sacred privilege, sporadic employment a fact of life, and the social welfare and law-enforcement agencies of the state, partners of one's existence.

The Bandit corner was subject to field observation for about three years—from June 1954 to May 1957. Hanging out on the corner during this period were six distinct but related gang subdivisions. There were four male groups: The Brigands, aged approximately 18 to 21 at the start of the study period; the Senior Bandits, aged 16 to 18; the Junior Bandits, 14 to 16, and the Midget Bandits, 12 to 14. There were also two distinct female subdivisions: The Bandettes, 14 to 16, and the Little Bandettes, 12 to 14.

The physical and psychic center of the Bandit corner was Sam's Variety Store, the owner and sole employee of which was not Sam but Ben, his son. Ben's father had founded the store in the 1920s, the heyday of the Irish laboring class in the Bandit neighborhood. When his father died, Ben took over the store, but did not change its name. Ben was a stocky, round-faced Jew in his middle fifties, who looked upon the whole of the Bandit neighborhood as his personal fief and bounden responsibility—a sacred legacy from his father. He knew everybody and was concerned with everybody; through his store passed a constant stream of customers and noncustomers of all ages and both sexes. In a space not much larger than that of a fair-sized bedroom Ben managed to crowd a phone booth, a juke box, a pinball machine, a space heater, counters, shelves and stock, and an assorted variety of patrons. During one 15-minute period on an average day Ben would supply $1.37 worth of groceries to 11-year-old Carol Donovan and enter the sum on her mother's page in the "tab" book, agree to extend Mrs. Thebodeau's already extended credit until her ADC check arrived, bandage and solace the three-year-old Negro girl who came crying to him with a cut forefinger, and shoo into the street a covey of Junior Bandits whose altercation over a pinball score was impeding customer traffic and augmenting an already substantial level of din.

Ben was a bachelor, and while he had adopted the whole of the Bandit neighborhood as his extended family, he had taken on the 200 adolescents who hung out on the Bandit corner as his most immediate sons and daughters. Ben knew the background and present circumstances of every Bandit, and followed their lives with intense interest and concern. Ben's corner-gang progeny were a fast-moving and mercurial lot, and he watched over their adventures and misadventures with a curious mixture of indignation, solicitude, disgust and sympathy. Ben's outlook on the affairs of the world was never bland; he held and freely voiced strong opinions on a wide variety of issues, prominent among which was the behavior and misbehavior of the younger generation.

This particular concern was given ample scope for attention by the young Bandits who congregated in and around his store. Of all the gangs studied, the Bandits were the most consistently and determinedly criminal, and central to Ben's concerns was how each one stood with regard to "trouble." In this respect, developments were seldom meager. By the time they reached the age of 18, every one of the 32 active members of the Senior Bandits had appeared in court at least once, and some many times; 28 of the 32 boys had been committed to a correctional institution and 16 had spent at least one term in confinement.

Ben's stout arm swept the expanse of pavement which fronted his store. "I'll tell ya, I give up on these kids. In all the years I been here, I never seen a worse bunch. You know what they should do? They should put up a big platform with one of them stocks right out there, and as soon as a kid gets in trouble, into the stocks with 'im. Then they'd straighten out. The way it is now, the kid tells a sob story to some soft-hearted cop or social worker, and pretty soon he's back at the same old thing. See that guy just comin' over here? That's what I mean. He's hopeless. Mark my word, he's gonna end up in the electric chair."

The Senior Bandit who entered the store came directly to Ben. "Hey, Ben, I just quit my job at the shoe factory. They don't pay ya nothin', and they got some wise guy nephew of the owner who thinks he can kick everyone around. I just got fed up. I ain't gonna tell Ma for awhile, she'll be mad." Ben's concern was evident. "Digger, ya just gotta learn you can't keep actin' smart to every boss ya have. And $1.30 an hour ain't bad pay at all for a 17-year-old boy. Look, I'll lend ya 10 bucks so ya can give 5 to ya Ma, and she won't know."

In their dealings with Ben, the Bandits, for their part, were in turn hostile and affectionate, cordial and sullen, open and reserved. They clearly regarded Ben's as "their" store. This meant, among other things, exclusive possession of the right to make trouble within its confines. At least three times during the observation period corner boys from outside neighborhoods entered the store obviously bent on stealing or creating a disturbance. On each occasion these outsiders were efficiently and forcefully removed by nearby Bandits, who then waxed indignant at the temerity of "outside" kids daring to consider Ben's as a target of illegal activity. One consequence, then, of Ben's seigneurial relationship to the Bandits was that his store was unusually well protected against theft, armed and otherwise, which presented a constant hazard to the small-store owner in Midcity.

On the other hand, the Bandits guarded jealously their

own right to raise hell in Ben's. On one occasion, several Senior Bandits came into the store with a cache of pistol bullets and proceeded to empty the powder from one of the bullets onto the pinball machine and to ignite the powder. When Ben ordered them out they continued operations on the front sidewalk by wrapping gunpowder in newspaper and igniting it. Finally they set fire to a wad of paper containing two live bullets which exploded and narrowly missed local residents sitting on nearby doorsteps.

Such behavior, while calculated to bedevil Ben and perhaps to retaliate for a recent scolding or ejection, posed no real threat to him or his store; the same boys during this period were actively engaged in serious thefts from similar stores in other neighborhoods. For the most part, the behavior of the Bandits in and around the store involved the characteristic activities of hanging out. In warm weather the Bandits sat outside the store on the sidewalk or doorstoops playing cards, gambling, drinking, talking to one another and to the Bandettes. In cooler weather they moved into the store as the hour and space permitted, and there played the pinball machine for such cash payoffs as Ben saw fit to render, danced with the Bandettes to juke box records, and engaged in general horseplay.

While Ben's was the Bandits' favorite hangout, they did frequent other hanging locales, mostly within a few blocks of the corner. Among these was a park directly adjacent to the housing project where the boys played football and baseball in season. At night the park provided a favored locale for activities such as beer drinking and lovemaking, neither of which particularly endeared them to the adult residents of the project, who not infrequently summoned the police to clear the park of late-night revellers. Other areas of congregation in the local neighborhood were a nearby delicatessen ("the Delly"), a pool hall, and the apartments of those Bandettes whose parents happened to be away. The Bandits also ran their own dances at the Old Erin and New Hibernia, but they had to conceal their identity as Bandits when renting these dance halls, since the proprietors had learned that the rental fees were scarcely sufficient to compensate for the chaos inevitably attending the conduct of a Bandit dance.

The Bandits were able to find other sources of entertainment in the central business district of Port City. While most of the Bandits and Bandettes were too young to gain admission to the numerous downtown cafes with their rock'n' roll bands, they were able to find amusement in going to the movies (sneaking in whenever possible), playing the coin machines in the penny arcades and shoplifting from the downtown department stores. Sometimes, as a kind of diversion, small groups of Bandits spent the day in town job-hunting, with little serious intention of finding work.

One especially favored form of downtown entertainment was the court trial. Members of the Junior and Senior Bandits performed as on-stage participants in some 250 court trials during a four-year period. Most trials involving juveniles were conducted in nearby Midcity Court as private proceedings, but the older Bandits had adopted as routine procedure the practice of appealing their local court sentences to the Superior Court located in downtown Port City. When the appeal was successful, it was the occasion for as large a turnout of gang members as could be mustered, and the Bandits were a rapt and vitally interested audience. Afterwards, the gang held long and animated discussions about the severity or leniency of the sentence and other, finer points of legal procedure. The hearings provided not only an absorbing form of free entertainment, but also invaluable knowledge about court functioning, appropriate defendant behavior, and the predilections of particular judges knowledge that would serve the spectators well when their own turn to star inevitably arrived.

The Senior Bandits

The Senior Bandits, the second oldest of the four male gang subdivisions hanging out on the Bandit corner, were under intensive observation for a period of 20 months. At the start of this period the boys ranged in age from 15 to 17 (average age 16.3) and at the end, 17 to 19 (average age 18.1). The core group of the Senior Bandits numbered 32 boys.

Most of the gang members were Catholic, the majority of Irish background; several were Italian or French Canadian, and a few were English or Scotch Protestants. The gang contained two sets of brothers and several cousins, and about one third of the boys had relatives in other subdivisions. These included a brother in the Midgets, six brothers in the Juniors, and three in the Marauders.

The educational and occupational circumstances of the Senior Bandits were remarkably like those of their parents. Some seven years after the end of the intensive study period, when the average age of the Bandits was 25, 23 out of the 27 gang members whose occupations were known held jobs ordinarily classified in the bottom two occupational categories of the United States census. Twenty-one were classified as "laborer," holding jobs such as roofer, stock boy and trucker's helper. Of 24 fathers whose occupations were known, 18, or 83 percent, held jobs in the same bottom two occupational categories as their sons; 17 were described as "laborer," holding jobs of similar kinds and in similar proportions to those of their sons, e.g., construction laborers: sons 30 percent, fathers 25 percent; factory laborers: sons 15 percent, fathers 21 percent. Clearly the Senior Bandits were not rising above their fathers' status. In fact, there were indications of a slight decline, even taking account of the younger age of the sons. Two of the boys' fathers held jobs in "public safety" services—one policeman and one fireman; another had worked for a time in the "white collar" position of a salesclerk at Sears; a fourth had risen to the rank of Chief Petty Officer in the Merchant Marine. Four of the fathers, in other words, had attained relatively elevated positions, while the sons produced only one policeman.

The education of the Senior Bandits was consistent with their occupational status. Of 29 boys whose educational experience was known, 27 dropped out of school in the eighth, ninth, or tenth grades, having reached the age of 16. Two did complete high school, and one of these was reputed to have taken some post-high-school training in a local technical school. None entered college. It should be remarked that this record occurred not in a backward rural community of the 1800s, nor in a black community, but in the 1950s in a predominantly white neighborhood of a metropolis that took pride in being one of the major educational centers of the world.

Since only two of the Senior Bandits were still in school during the study, almost all of the boys held full-time jobs at some time during the contact period. But despite financial needs, pressure from parents and parole officers and other incentives to get work, the Senior Bandits found jobs slowly, accepted them reluctantly, and quit them with little provocation.

The Senior Bandits were clearly the most criminal of the seven gangs we studied most closely. For example, by the time he had reached the age of 18 the average Senior Bandit had been charged with offenses in court an average of 7.6 times; this compared with an average rate of 2.7 for all five male gangs, and added up to a total of almost 250 separate charges for the gang as a whole. A year after our intensive contact with the group, 100 percent of the

Senior Bandits had been arrested at least once, compared with an average arrest figure of 45 percent for all groups. During the 20-month contact period, just about half of the Senior Bandits were on probation or parole for some period of time.

To a greater degree than in any of the other gangs we studied, crime as an occupation and preoccupation played a central role in the lives of the Senior Bandits. Prominent among recurrent topics of discussion were thefts successfully executed, fights recently engaged in, and the current status of gang members who were in the process of passing through the successive states of arrest, appearing in court, being sentenced, appealing, re-appealing and so on. Although none of the crimes of the Senior Bandits merited front-page headlines when we were close to them, a number of their more colorful exploits did receive newspaper attention, and the stories were carefully clipped and left in Ben's store for circulation among the gang members. Newspaper citations functioned for the Senior Bandits somewhat as do press notices for actors; gang members who made the papers were elated and granted prestige; those who did not were often disappointed; participants and non-participants who failed to see the stories felt cheated.

The majority of their crimes were thefts. The Senior Bandits were thieves par excellence, and their thievery was imaginative, colorful and varied. Most thefts were from stores. Included among these was a department store theft of watches, jewelry and clothing for use as family Christmas presents; a daylight raid on a supermarket for food and refreshments needed for a beach outing; a daytime burglary of an antique store, in which eight gang members, in the presence of the owner, stole a Samurai sword and French duelling pistols. The gang also engaged in car theft. One summer several Bandits stole a car to visit girl friends who were working at a summer resort. Sixty miles north of Port City, hailed by police for exceeding speed limits, they raced away at speeds of up to 100 miles an hour, overturned the car, and were hospitalized for injuries. In another instance, Bandits stole a car in an effort to return a drunken companion to his home and avoid the police; when this car stalled they stole a second one parked in front of its owner's house; the owner ran out and fired several shots at the thieves, which, however, failed to forestall the theft.

The frequency of Senior Bandit crimes, along with the relative seriousness of their offenses, resulted in a high rate of arrest and confinement. During the contact period somewhat over 40 percent of the gang members were confined in correctional institutions, with terms averaging 11 months per boy. The average Senior Bandit spent approximately one month out of four in a correctional facility. This circumstance prompted one of the Bandettes to remark, "Ya know, them guys got a new place to hang—the reformatory. That bunch is never together—one halfa them don't even know the other half. . . ."

This appraisal, while based on fact, failed to recognize an important feature of gang relationships. With institutional confinement a frequent and predictable event, the Senior Bandits employed a set of devices to maintain a high degree of group solidarity. Lines of communication between corner and institution were kept open by frequent visits by those on the outside, during which inmates were brought food, money and cigarettes as well as news of the neighborhood and other correctional facilities. One Midcity social worker claimed that the institutionalized boys knew what was going on in the neighborhood before most neighborhood residents. The Bandits also developed well-established methods for arranging and carrying out institutional escape by those gang members who were so inclined. Details of escapes were arranged in the course of visits and inter-inmate contacts; escapees were provided by fellow gang members with equipment such as ropes to scale prison walls and getaway cars. The homes of one's gang fellows were also made available as hideouts. Given this set of arrangements, the Bandits carried out several highly successful escapes, and one succeeded in executing the first escape in the history of a maximum security installation.

The means by which the Senior Bandits achieved group cohesion in spite of recurrent incarcerations of key members merit further consideration—both because they are of interest in their own right, and because they throw light on important relationships between leadership, group structure, and the motivation of criminal behavior. Despite the assertion that "one halfa them guys don't know the other half," the Senior Bandits were a solidaristic associational unit, with clear group boundaries and definite criteria for differentiating those who were "one of us" from those who were not. It was still said of an accepted group member that "he hangs with us"—even when the boy had been away from the corner in an institution for a year or more. Incarcerated leaders, in particular, were referred to frequently and in terms of admiration and respect.

The system used by the Senior Bandits to maintain solidarity and reliable leadership arrangements incorporated three major devices: the diffusion of authority, anticipation of contingencies and interchangeability of roles. The recurring absence from the corner of varying numbers of gang members inhibited the formation of a set of relatively stable cliques of the kind found in the other gangs we studied intensively. What was fairly stable, instead, was a set of "classes" of members, each of which could include different individuals at different times. The relative size of these classes was fairly constant, and a member of one class could move to another to take the place of a member who had been removed by institutionalization.

The four major classes of gang members could be called key leaders, standby leaders, primary followers and secondary followers. During the intensive contact period the gang contained five key leaders—boys whose accomplishments had earned them the right to command; six standby leaders—boys prepared to step into leadership positions when key leaders were institutionalized; eight primary followers—boys who hung out regularly and who were the most dependable followers of current leaders; and 13 secondary followers—boys who hung out less regularly and who tended to adapt their allegiances to particular leadership situations.

Predictably, given the dominant role of criminal activity among the Senior Bandits, leadership and followership were significantly related to criminal involvement. Each of the five key leaders had demonstrated unusual ability in criminal activity; in this respect the Senior Bandits differed from the other gangs, each of which included at least one leader whose position was based in whole or in part on a commitment to a law-abiding course of action. One of the Senior Bandits' key leaders was especially respected for his daring and adeptness in theft; another, who stole infrequently relative to other leaders, for his courage, stamina and resourcefulness as a fighter. The other three leaders had proven themselves in both theft and fighting, with theft the more important basis of eminence.

Confinement statistics show that gang members who were closet to leadership positions were also the most active in crime. They also suggest, however, that maintaining a system of leadership on this basis poses special problems. The more criminally active a gang member, the greater the likelihood that he would be apprehended and removed from the neighborhood, thus substantially diminishing his opportunities to convert earning prestige into operative leadership. How was it possible, then, for the Senior Bandits to maintain effective leadership arrangements? They utilized a remarkably efficient system whose several features were ingenious and deftly contrived.

First, the recognition by the Bandits of five key leaders—a relatively large number for a gang of 32 members—served as a form of insurance against being left without leadership. It was most unlikely that all five would be incarcerated at the same time, particularly since collective crimes were generally executed by one or possibly two leaders along with several of their followers. During one relatively brief part of the contact period, four of the key leaders were confined simultaneously, but over the full period the average number confined at any one time was two. One Bandit key leader expressed his conviction that exclusive reliance on a single leader was unwise: ". . . since we been hangin' out [at Ben's corner] we ain't had no leader. Other kids got a leader of the gang. Like up in Cornerville, they always got one kid who's the big boss . . . so far we ain't did that, and I don't think we ever will. We talk about 'Smiley and his boys,' or 'Digger and his clique,' and like that. . . ."

It is clear that for this Bandit the term "leader" carried the connotation of a single and all-powerful gang lord, which was not applicable to the diffuse and decentralized leadership arrangements of the Bandits. It is also significant that the gangs of Cornerville which he used as an example were Italian gangs whose rate of criminal involvement was relatively low. The "one big boss" type of leadership found in these gangs derives from the "Caesar" or "Il Duce" pattern so well established in Italian culture, and it was workable for Cornerville gangs because the gangs and their leaders were sufficiently law-abiding and /or sufficiently capable of evading arrest as to make the removal of the leader an improbable event.

A second feature of Bandit leadership, the use of "stand-by" leaders, made possible a relatively stable balance among the several cliques. When the key leader of his clique was present in the area, the standby leader assumed a subordinate role and did not initiate action; if and when the key leader was committed to an institution, the standby was ready to assume leadership. He knew, however, that he was expected to relinquish this position on the return of the key leader. By this device each of the five major cliques was assured some form of leadership even when key leaders were absent, and could maintain its form, identity and influence vis-a-vis other cliques.

A third device that enabled the gang to maintain a relatively stable leadership and clique structure involved the phenomenon of "optimal" criminal involvement. Since excellence in crime was the major basis of gang leadership, it might be expected that some of those who aspired to leadership would assume that there was a simple and direct relationship between crime and leadership: the more crime, the more prestige; the more prestige, the stronger the basis of authority. The flaw in this simple formula was in fact recognized by the actual key leaders: in striving for maximal criminal involvement, one also incurred the maximum risk of incarceration. But leadership involved more than gaining prestige through crime; one had to be personally involved with other gang members for sufficiently extended periods to exploit won prestige through wooing followers, initiating noncriminal as well as criminal activities, and effecting working relationships with other leaders. Newly-returned key leaders as well as the less criminally-active class of standby leaders tended to step up their involvement in criminal activity on assuming or reassuming leadership positions in order to solidify their positions, but they also tended to diminish such involvement once this was achieved.

One fairly evident weakness in so flexible and fluid a system of cliques and leadership was the danger that violent and possibly disruptive internal conflict might erupt among key leaders who were competing for followers, or standby leaders who were reluctant to relinquish their positions. There was, in fact, surprisingly little overt conflict of any kind among Bandit leaders. On their release from confinement, leaders were welcomed with enthusiasm and appropriate observances both by their followers and by other leaders. They took the center of the stage as they recounted to rapt listeners their institutional experiences, the circumstances of those still confined, and new developments in policies, personnel and politics at the correctional school.

When they were together Bandit leaders dealt with one another gingerly, warily and with evident respect. On one occasion a standby leader, who was less criminally active than the returning key leader, offered little resistance to being displaced, but did serve his replacement with the warning that a resumption of his former high rate of crime would soon result in commitment both of himself and his clique. On another occasion one of the toughest of the Senior Bandits (later sentenced to an extended term in an adult institution for ringleading a major prison riot), returned to the corner to find that another leader had taken over not only some of his key followers but his steady girl friend as well. Instead of taking on his rival in an angry and perhaps violent confrontation, he reacted quite mildly, venting his hostility in the form of sarcastic teasing, calculated to needle but not to incite. In the place of a direct challenge, the newly returned key leader set about to regain his followers and his girl by actively throwing himself back into criminal activity. This course of action—competing for followers by successful performance in prestigious activities rather than by brute-force confrontation—was standard practice among the Senior Bandits.

The Junior Bandits

The leadership system of the Junior Bandits was, if anything, even farther removed from the "one big boss" pattern than was the "multi-leader power-balance" system of the Seniors. An intricate arrangement of cliques and leadership enabled this subdivision of the gang to contain within it a variety of individuals and cliques with different and often conflicting orientations.

Leadership for particular activities was provided as the occasion arose by boys whose competence in that activity had been established. Leadership was thus flexible, shifting and adaptable to changing group circumstances. Insofar as there was a measure of relatively concentrated authority, it was invested in a collectivity rather than an individual. The several "situational" leaders of the dominant clique constituted what was in effect a kind of ruling council, which arrived at its decisions through a process of extended collective discussion generally involving all concerned. Those who were to execute a plan of action thereby took part in the process by which it was developed.

A final feature of this system concerns the boy who was recognized as "the leader" of the Junior Bandits. When the gang formed a club to expedite involvement in athletic activities, he was chosen its president. Although he was an accepted member of the dominant clique, he did not, on the surface, seem to possess any particular qualifications for this position. He was mild-mannered, unassertive, and consistently refused to take a definite stand on outstanding issues, let alone taking the initiative in implementing policy. He appeared to follow rather than to lead. One night when the leaders of the two subordinate factions became infuriated with one another in the course of a dispute, he trailed both boys around for several hours, begging them to calm down and reconcile their differences. On another occasion the gang was on the verge of splitting into irreconcilable factions over a financial issue. One group accused another of stealing club funds; the accusation was hotly denied; angry recriminations arose that swept in a variety of dissatisfactions with the club and its conduct. In the course of this melee, the leader of one faction, the "bad boys," complained bitterly about the refusal of the president to take sides or assume any initiative in resolving the dispute, and called for a new election. This was agreed to and the election was held—with the result that the "weak" president was re-elected by a decisive majority, and was reinstated in office amidst emotional outbursts of acclaim and reaffirmation of the unity of the gang.

It was thus evident that the majority of gang members, despite temporary periods of anger over particular issues, recognized on some level the true function performed by a "weak" leader. Given the fact that the gang included a set of cliques with differing orientations and conflicting notions, and a set of leaders whose authority was limited to specific areas, the maintenance of gang cohesion required some special mechanisms. One was the device of the "weak" leader. It is most unlikely that a forceful or dominant person could have controlled the sanctions that would enable him to coerce the strong-willed factions into compliance. The very fact that the "weak" leader refused to take sides and was noncommittal on key issues made him acceptable to the conflicting interests represented in the gang. Further, along with the boy's nonassertive demeanor went a real talent for mediation.

The Outlaw Neighborhood

The Outlaw street corner was less than a mile from that of the Bandits, and like the Bandits, the Outlaws were white, Catholic, and predominantly Irish, with a few Italians and Irish-Italians. But their social status, in the middle range of the lower class, was sufficiently higher than that of the Bandits to be reflected in significant differences in both their gang and family life. The neighborhood environment also was quite different.

Still, the Outlaws hung out on a classic corner—complete with drug store, variety store, a neighborhood bar (Callahan's Bar and Grill), a pool hall and several other small businesses such as a laundromat. The corner was within one block of a large park, a convenient locale for card games, lovemaking and athletic practice. Most residents of the Outlaw neighborhood were oblivious to the deafening roar of the elevated train that periodically rattled the houses and stores of Midcity Avenue, which formed one street of the Outlaw corner. There was no housing project in the Outlaw neighborhood, and none of the Outlaws were project residents. Most of their families rented one level of one of the three-decker wooden tenements which were common in the area; a few owned their own homes.

In the mid-1950s, however, the Outlaw neighborhood underwent significant changes as Negroes began moving in. Most of the white residents, gradually and with reluctance, left their homes and moved out to the first fringe of Port City's residential suburbs, abandoning the area to the Negroes.

Prior to this time the Outlaw corner had been a hanging locale for many years. The Outlaw name and corner dated from at least the late 1920s, and perhaps earlier. One local boy who was not an Outlaw observed disgruntledly that anyone who started a fight with an Outlaw would end up fighting son, father and grandfather, since all were or had been members of the gang. A somewhat drunken and sentimental Outlaw, speaking at a farewell banquet for their field worker, declared impassionedly that any infant born into an Outlaw family was destined from birth to wear the Outlaw jacket.

One consequence of the fact that Outlaws had hung out on the same corner for many years was that the group that congregated there during the 30-month observation period included a full complement of age-graded subdivisions. Another consequence was that the subdivisions were closely connected by kinship. There were six clearly differentiated subdivisions on the corner: the Marauders, boys in their late teens and early twenties; the Senior Outlaws, boys between 16 and 18; the Junior Outlaws, 14 to 16; and the Midget Outlaws, 11 to 13. There were also two girls groups, the Outlawettes and the Little Outlawettes. The number of Outlaws in all subdivisions totalled slightly over 200 persons, ranging in age, approximately, from 10 to 25 years.

The cohesiveness of the Outlaws, during the 1950s, was enhanced in no small measure by an adult who, like Ben for the Bandits, played a central role in the Outlaws' lives. This was Rosa—the owner of the variety store which was their principal hangout—a stout, unmarried woman of about 40 who was, in effect, the street-corner mother of all 200 Outlaws.

The Junior Outlaws

The Junior Outlaws, numbering 24 active members, were the third oldest of the four male subdivisions on the Outlaw Corner, ranging in age from 14 to 16. Consistent with their middle-range lower-class status, the boys' fathers were employed in such jobs as bricklayer, mechanic, chauffeur, milk deliveryman; but a small minority of these men had attained somewhat higher positions, one being the owner of a small electroplating shop and the other rising to the position of plant superintendent. The educational status of the Junior Outlaws was higher than that of the Bandit gangs, but lower than that of their older brother gang, the Senior Outlaws.

With regard to law violations, the Junior Outlaws, as one might expect from their status and age, were considerably less criminal than the lower-status Bandits, but considerably more so than the Senior Outlaws. They ranked third among the five male gangs in illegal involvement during the observation period (25 involvements per 10 boys per 10 months), which was well below the second-ranking Senior Bandits (54.2) and well above the fourth-ranking Negro Kings (13.9). Nevertheless, the two-and-a-half-year period during which we observed the Juniors was for them, as for other boys of their status and age group, a time of substantial increase in the frequency and seriousness of illegal behavior. An account of the events of this time provides some insight into the process by which age-related influences engender criminality. It also provides another variation on the issue, already discussed in the case of the Bandits, of the relation of leadership to criminality.

It is clear from the case of the Bandits that gang affairs were ordered not by autocratic ganglords, but rather through a subtle and intricate interplay between leadership and a set of elements such as personal competency, intra-gang divisions and law violation. The case of the Junior Outlaws is particularly dramatic in this regard, since the observation period found them at the critical age when boys of this social-status level are faced with a serious decision—the amount of weight to be granted to law-violating behavior as a basis of prestige. Because there were in the Junior Outlaws two cliques, each of which was committed quite clearly to opposing alternatives, the interplay of the various elements over time emerges with some vividness, and echoes the classic morality play wherein forces of good and evil are locked in mortal combat over the souls of the uncommitted.

At the start of the observation period, the Juniors, 13-,

14-and 15-year-olds, looked and acted for the most part like "nice young kids." By the end of the period both their voices and general demeanor had undergone a striking change. Their appearance, as they hung out in front of Rosa's store, was that of rough corner boys, and the series of thefts, fights and drinking bouts which had occurred during the intervening two-and-one-half years was the substance behind that appearance. When we first contacted them, the Juniors comprised three main cliques; seven boys associated primarily with a "good boy" who was quite explicitly oriented to law-abiding behavior; a second clique of seven boys associated with a "bad boy" who was just starting to pursue prestige through drinking and auto theft; and a third, less-frequently congregating group, who took a relatively neutral position with respect to the issue of violative behavior.

The leader of the "good boy" clique played an active part in the law-abiding activities of the gang, and was elected president of the formal club organized by the Juniors. This club at first included members of all three cliques; however, one of the first acts of the club members, dominated by the "good boy" leader and his supporters, was to vote out of membership the leader of the "bad boy" clique. Nevertheless, the "bad boy" leader and his followers continued to hang out on the corner with the other Juniors, and from this vantage point attempted to gain influence over the uncommitted boys as well as members of the "good boy" clique. His efforts proved unsuccessful, however, since during this period athletic prowess served for the majority of the Juniors as a basis of greater prestige than criminal behavior. Disgruntled by this failure, the "bad boy" leader took his followers and moved to a new hanging corner, about two blocks away from the traditional one.

From there, a tangible symbol of the ideological split

within the Juniors, the "bad boy" leader continued his campaign to wean away the followers of the "good boy" leader, trying to persuade them to leave the old corner for the new. At the same time, behavior at the "bad boy" corner became increasingly delinquent, with, among other things, much noisy drinking and thefts of nearby cars. These incidents produced complaints by local residents that resulted in several police raids on the corner, and served to increase the antagonism between what now had become hostile factions. Determined to assert their separateness, the "bad boy" faction began to drink and create disturbances in Rosa's store, became hostile to her when she censured them, and finally stayed away from the store altogether.

The antagonism between the two factions finally became sufficiently intense to bring about a most unusual circumstance—plans for an actual gang fight, a "jam" of the type characteristic of rival gangs. The time and place for the battle were agreed on. But no one from either side showed up. A second battle site was selected. Again the combatants failed to appear. From the point of view of intragang relations, both the plan for the gang fight and its failure to materialize were significant. The fact that a physical fight between members of the same subdivision was actually projected showed that factional hostility over the issue of law violation had reached an unusual degree of bitterness; the fact that the planned encounters did not in fact occur indicated a realization that actual physical combat might well lead to an irreversible split.

A reunification of the hostile factions did not take place for almost a year, however. During this time changes occurred in both factions which had the net effect of blunting the sharpness of the ideological issues dividing them. Discouraged by his failure to win over the majority of the Outlaws to the cause of law-violation as a major badge of prestige, the leader of the "bad boy" clique began to hang out less frequently. At the same time, the eight "uncommitted" members of the Junior Outlaws, now moving toward their middle teens, began to gravitate toward the "bad boy" corner—attracted by the excitement and risk of its activities. More of the Juniors than ever before became involved in illegal drinking and petty theft. This trend became sufficiently pronounced to draw in members of the "good boy" clique, and the influence of the "good boy" leader diminished to the point where he could count on the loyalty only of his own brother and two other boys. In desperation, sensing the all-but-irresistible appeal of illegality for his erstwhile followers, he increased the tempo of his own delinquent behavior in a last-ditch effort to win them back. All in vain. Even his own brother deserted the regular Outlaw corner, although he did not go so far as to join the "bad boys" on theirs.

Disillusioned, the "good boy" leader took a night job that sharply curtailed the time he was able to devote to gang activities. Members of the "bad boy" clique now began a series of maneuvers aimed at gaining control of the formal club. Finally, about two months before the close of the 30-month contact period, a core member of the "bad boy" clique was elected to the club presidency. In effect, the proponents of illegality as a major basis of prestige had won the long struggle for dominance of the Junior Outlaws. But this achievement, while on the surface a clear victory for the "bad boy" faction, was in fact a far more subtle process of mutual accommodation.

The actions of each of the opposing sides accorded quite directly with their expressed convictions; each member of the "bad boy" faction averaged about 17 known illegal acts during the observation period, compared to a figure of about two per boy for the "good boy" faction. However, in the face of these sharp differences in both actions and sentiments respecting illegality, the two factions shared important common orientations. Most importantly, they shared the conviction that the issue of violative behavior as a basis of prestige was a paramount one, and one that required a choice. Moreover, both sides remained uncertain as to whether the choice they made was the correct one.

The behavior of both factions provides evidence of a fundamental ambivalence with respect to the "demanded" nature of delinquent behavior. The gradual withdrawal of support by followers of the "good boy" leader and the movement toward violative behavior of the previously "neutral" clique attest to a compelling conviction that prestige gained through law-abiding endeavor alone could not, at this age, suffice. Even more significant was the criminal experience of the "good boy" leader. As the prime exponent of law-abiding behavior, he might have been expected to serve as an exemplar in this respect. In fact, the opposite was true; his rate of illegal involvement was the highest of all the boys in his clique, and had been so even before his abortive attempt to regain his followers by a final burst of delinquency. This circumstance probably derived from his realization that a leader acceptable to both factions (which he wanted to be) would have to show proficiency in activities recognized by both as conferring prestige.

It is equally clear, by the same token, that members of the "bad boy" faction were less than serenely confident in their commitment to law-violation as an ideal. Once they had won power in the club they did not keep as their leader the boy who had been the dominant figure on the "bad boy" corner, and who was without question the most criminally active of the Junior Outlaws, but instead elected as president another boy who was also criminally active, but considerably less so. Moreover, in the presence of older gang members, Seniors and Marauders, the "bad boy" clique was far more subdued, less obstreperous, and far less ardent in their advocacy of crime as an ideal. There was little question that they were sensitive to and responsive to negative reactions by others to their behavior.

It is noteworthy that members of both factions adhered more firmly to the "law-violation" and "law-abiding" positions on the level of abstract ideology than on the level of actual practice. This would suggest that the existence of the opposing ideologies and their corresponding factions served important functions both for individual gang members and for the group as a whole. Being in the same orbit as the "bad boys" made it possible for the "good boys" to reap some of the rewards of violative behavior without undergoing its risks; the presence of the "good boys" imposed restraints on the "bad" that they themselves desired, and helped protect them from dangerous excesses. The behavior and ideals of the "good boys" satisfied for both factions that component of their basic orientation that said "violation of the law is wrong and should be punished;" the behavior and ideals of the "bad boys" that component that said "one cannot earn manhood without some involvement in criminal activity."

It is instructive to compare the stress and turmoil attending the struggle for dominance of the Junior Outlaws with the leadership circumstances of the Senior Bandits. In this gang, older and of lower social status (lower-class III), competition for leadership had little to do with a choice between law-abiding and law-violating philosophies, but rather with the issue of which of a number of competing leaders was *best* able to demonstrate prowess in illegal activity. This virtual absence of effective pressures against delinquency contrasts sharply with the situation of the Junior Outlaws. During the year-long struggle between its "good" and "bad" factions, the Juniors were exposed to constant pressures, both internal and external to the gang, to refrain from illegality. External sources included Rosa, whom the boys loved and respected; a local youth worker whom they held in high esteem; their older brother gangs, whose frequent admonitions to the "little kids" to "straighten out" and "keep clean" were attended with utmost seriousness. Within the gang itself the "good boy" leader served as a consistent and persuasive advocate of a lawabiding course of action. In addition, most of the boys' parents deplored their misbehavior and urged them to keep out of trouble.

In the face of all these pressures from persons of no small importance in the lives of the Juniors, the final triumph of the proponents of illegality, however tempered, assumes added significance. What was it that impelled the "bad boy" faction? There was a quality of defiance about much of their delinquency, as if they were saying—"We know perfectly well that what we are doing is regarded as wrong, legally and morally; we also know that it violates the wishes and standards of many whose good opinion we value; yet, if we are to sustain our self-respect and our honor as males we *must*, at this stage of our lives, engage in criminal behavior." In light of the experience of the Junior Outlaws, one can scarcely argue that their delinquency sprang from any inability to distinguish right from wrong, or out of any simple conformity to a set of parochial standards that just happened to differ from those of the legal code or the adult middle class. Their delinquent behavior was engendered by a highly complex interplay of forces, including, among other elements, the fact that they were males, were in the middle range of the lower class and of critical importance in the present instance, were moving through the age period when the attainment of manhood was of the utmost concern.

In the younger gang just discussed, the Junior Outlaws, leadership and clique structure reflected an intense struggle between advocates and opponents of law-violation as a prime basis of prestige.

The Senior Outlaws

Leadership in the older Senior Outlaws reflected a resolution of the law-conformity versus law-violation conflict, but with different results. Although the gang was not under direct observation during their earlier adolescence, what we know of the Juniors, along with evidence that the Senior Outlaws themselves had been more criminal when younger, would suggest that the gang had in fact undergone a similar struggle and that the proponents of conformity to the law had won.

In any case, the events of the observation period made it clear that the Senior Outlaws sought "rep" as a gang primarily through effective execution of legitimate enterprises such as athletics, dances, and other non-violative activities. In line with this objective, they maintained a consistent concern with the "good name" of the gang and with "keeping out of trouble" in the face of constant and ubiquitous temptations. For example, they attempted (without much success) to establish friendly relations with the senior priest of their parish—in contrast with the Junior Outlaws, who were on very bad terms with the local church. At one point during the contact period when belligerent Bandits, claiming that the Outlaws had attacked one of the Midget Bandits, vowed to "wipe out every Outlaw jacket in Midcity," the Senior Outlaws were concerned not only with the threat of attack but also with the threat to their reputation. "That does it," said one boy, "I knew we'd get into something. There goes the good name of the Outlaws."

Leadership and clique arrangements in the Senior Outlaws reflected three conditions, each related in some way to the relatively low stress on criminal activity: the stability of gang membership (members were rarely removed from the area by institutional confinement), the absence of significant conflict over the prestige and criminality issue, and the importance placed on legitimate collective activities. The Senior Bandits were the most unified of the gangs we observed directly; there were no important cleavages or factions; even the distinction between more-active and less-active members was less pronounced than in the other gangs.

But as in the other gangs, leadership among the Senior Outlaws was collective and situational. There were four key leaders, each of whom assumed authority in his own sphere of competence. As in the case of the Bandit gangs there was little overt competition among leaders; when differences arose between the leadership and the rank and file, the several leaders tended to support one another. In one significant respect, however, Outlaw leadership differed from that of the other gangs; authority was exercised more firmly and accepted more readily. Those in charge of collective enterprises generally issued commands after the manner of a tough army sergeant or work-gang boss. Although obedience to such commands was frequently less than flawless, the leadership style of Outlaw leaders approximated the "snap-to-it" approach of organizations that control firmer sanctions than do most corner gangs. Compared to the near-chaotic behavior of their younger brother gang, the organizational practices of the Senior appeared as a model of efficiency. The "authoritarian" mode of leadership was particularly characteristic of one boy, whose perogatives were somewhat more generalized than those of the other leaders. While he was far from an undisputed "boss," holding instead a kind of *primus inter pares* position, he was as close to a "boss" as anything found among the direct-observation gangs.

His special position derived from the fact that he showed superior capability in an unusually wide range of activities, and this permitted him wider authority than the other leaders. One might have expected, in a gang oriented predominantly to law-abiding activity, that this leader would serve as an exemplar of legitimacy and rank among the most law-abiding. This was not the case. He was, in fact, one of the most criminal of the Senior Outlaws, being among the relatively few who had "done time." He was a hard drinker, an able street-fighter, a skilled football strategist and team leader, an accomplished dancer and smooth ladies' man. His leadership position was based not on his capacity to best exemplify the law-abiding orientation of the gang, but on his capabilities in a variety of activities, violative and non-violative. Thus, even in the gang most concerned with "keeping clean," excellence in crime still constituted one important basis of prestige. Competence as such rather than the legitimacy of one's activities provided the major basis of authority.

We still have to ask, however, why leadership among the Senior Outlaws was more forceful than in the other gangs. One reason emerges by comparison with the "weak leader" situation of the Junior Bandits. Younger and of lower social status, their factional conflict over the law-violation-and-prestige issue was sufficiently intense so that only a leader without an explicit commitment to either side could be acceptable to both. The Seniors, older and of higher status, had developed a good degree of intragang consensus on this issue, and showed little factionalism. They could thus accept a relatively strong leader without jeopardizing gang unity.

A second reason also involves differences in age and social status, but as these relate to the world of work. In contrast to the younger gangs, whose perspectives more directly revolved around the subculture of adolescence and its specific concerns, the Senior Outlaws at age 19 were on the threshold of adult work, and some in fact were actively engaged in it. In contrast to the lower-status gangs whose orientation to gainful employment was not and never would be as "responsible" as that of the Outlaws, the activities of the Seniors as gang members more directly reflected and anticipated the requirements and conditions of the adult occupational roles they would soon assume.

Of considerable importance in the prospective occupational world of the Outlaws was, and is, the capacity to give and take orders in the execution of collective enterprises. Unlike the Bandits, few of whom would ever occupy other than subordinate positions, the Outlaws belonged to that sector of society which provides the men who exercise direct authority over groups of laborers or blue collar workers. The self-executed collective activities of the gang—organized athletics, recreational projects, fund-raising activities—provided a training ground for the practice of organizational skills—planning organized enterprises, working together in their conduct, executing the directives of legitimate superiors. It also provided a training ground wherein those boys with the requisite talents could learn and practice the difficult art of exercising authority effectively over lower-class men. By the time they had reached the age of twenty, the leaders of the Outlaws had experienced in the gang many of the problems and responsibilities confronting the army sergeant, the police lieutenant and the factory foreman.

The nature and techniques of leadership in the Senior Outlaws had relevance not only to their own gang but to the Junior Outlaws as well. Relations between the Junior and Senior Outlaws were the closest of all the intensive-contact gang subdivisions. The Seniors kept a close watch on their younger fellows, and served them in a variety of ways, as athletic coaches, advisers, mediators and arbiters. The older gang followed the factional conflicts of the Juniors with close attention, and were not above intervening when conflict reached sufficient intensity or threatened their own interests. The dominant leader of the Seniors was particularly concerned with the behavior of the Juniors; at one point, lecturing them about their disorderly conduct in Rosa's store, he remarked. "I don't hang with you guys, but I know what you do. . . ." The Seniors did not, however, succeed in either preventing the near-breakup of the Junior Outlaws or slowing their move toward law-breaking activities.

The Prevalence of Gangs

The subtle and intricately contrived relations among cliques, leadership and crime in the four subdivisions of the Bandits and Outlaws reveal the gang as an ordered and adaptive form of association, and its members as able and rational human beings. The fascinating pattern of inter-gang variation within a basic framework illustrates vividly the compelling influences of differences in age and social status on crime, leadership and other forms of behavior— even when these differences are surprisingly small. The experiences of Midcity gang members show that the gang serves the lower-class adolescent as a flexible and adaptable training instrument for imparting vital knowledge concerning the value of individual competence, the appropriate limits of law-violating behavior, the uses and abuses of authority, and the skills of interpersonal relations. From this perspective, the street gang appears not as a casual or transient manifestation that emerges intermittently in response to unique and passing social conditions, but rather as a stable associational form, coordinate with and complementary to the family, and as an intrinsic part of the way of life of the urban low-status community.

How then can one account for the widespread conception of gangs as somehow popping up and then disappearing again? One critical reason concerns the way one defines what a gang is. Many observers, both scholars and non-scholars, often use a *sine qua non* to sort out "real" gangs from near-gangs, pseudo-gangs, and non-gangs. Among the more common of these single criteria are: autocratic one-man leadership, some "absolute" degree of solidarity or stable membership, a predominant involvement in violent conflict with other gangs, claim to a rigidly defined turf, or participation in activities thought to pose a threat to other sectors of the community. Reaction to groups lacking the *sine qua non* is often expressed with a dismissive "Oh, them. That's not a *gang*. That's just a bunch of kids out on the corner."

For many people there are no gangs if there is no gang warfare. It's that simple. For them, as for all those who concentrate on the "threatening" nature of the gang, the phenomenon is defined in terms of the degree of "problem" it poses: A group whose "problematic" behavior is hard to ignore is a gang; one less problematic is not. But what some people see as a problem may not appear so to others. In Philadelphia, for example, the police reckoned there were 80 gangs, of which 20 were at war; while social workers estimated there were 200 gangs, of which 80 were "most hostile." Obviously, the social workers' 80 "most hostile" gangs were the same as the 80 "gangs" of the police. The additional 120 groups defined as gangs by the social workers were seen as such because they were thought to be appropriate objects of social work; but to the police they were not sufficiently troublesome to require consistent police attention, and were not therefore defined as gangs.

In view of this sort of confusion, let me state our definition of what a gang is. A gang is a group of urban adolescents who congregate recurrently at one or more nonresidential locales, with continued affiliation based on self-defined criteria of inclusion and exclusion. Recruitment, customary places of assembly and ranging areas are based in a specific territory, over some portion of which limited use and occupancy rights are claimed. Membership both in the gang as a whole and in its subgroups is determined on the basis of age. The group maintains a versatile repertoire of activities, with hanging out, mating, recreational and illegal activity being of central importance; and it is internally differentiated on the basis of authority, prestige, personality and clique-formation.

The main reason that people have consistently mistaken the prevalence of gangs is the widespread tendency to define them as gangs on the basis of the presence or absence of one or two characteristics that are thought to be essential to the "true" gang. Changes in the forms or frequencies or particular characteristics, such as leadership, involvement in fighting, or modes of organization, are seen not as normal variations over time and space, but rather as signs of the emergence or disappearance of the gangs themselves. Our work does not support this view; instead, our evidence indicates that the core characteristics of the gang vary continuously from place to place and from time to time without negating the existence of the gang. Gangs may be larger or smaller, named or nameless, modestly or extensively differentiated, more or less active in gang fighting, stronger or weaker in leadership, black, white, yellow or brown, without affecting their identity as gangs. So long as groups of adolescents gather periodically outside the home, frequent a particular territory, restrict membership by age and other criteria, pursue a variety of activities, and maintain differences in authority and prestige—so long will the gang continue to exist as a basic associational form.

September 1969

FURTHER READING:

The Gang: A Study of 1313 Gangs in Chicago by Frederic M. Thrasher (Chicago: University of Chicago Press, 1927) is the classic work on American youth gangs. Although published in the 1920s, it remains the most detailed and comprehensive treatise on gangs and gang life ever written.

Delinquent Boys: The Culture of the Gang by Albert K. Cohen (Glencoe, Ill.: Free Press, 1955) is the first-major attempt to explain the behavior of gang members using modern sociological theory.

Delinquency and Opportunity: A Theory of Delinquent Gangs by Richard A. Cloward and Lloyd E. Ohlin (Glencoe, Ill.: Free Press, 1960) explains the existence, both of gangs, and major types of gangs. It has had a profound impact on American domestic policy.

Group Process and Gang Delinquency by James F. Short Jr. and Fred L. Strodtbeck (Chicago: University of Chicago Press, 1965). An empirical "test" of divergent theories of gangs and delinquency, it includes the first extensive application of statistical techniques and the first systematic application of the social-psychological conceptual framework to the study of gangs.

Homeless Men

DAVID J. PITTMAN

In the early days of urban redevelopment some American cities tried to eliminate their skid row areas with bulldozers. The assumption was that skid rows were only collections of obsolescent buildings. Much to the surprise of the planners, skid rows which had previously been confined to one or two areas in each city divided and multiplied, reappearing in many new locations.

When Philadelphia and Chicago, therefore, planned redevelopment for their skid rows, they called in social scientists from Temple University and the National Opinion Research Center to provide reliable data on which to make decisions concerning the relocation of the skid row population.

This experience in urban redevelopment points to the need for more systematic research in urban sociology to study the historical development of skid rows and the social and economic forces that continue the pattern. For the fact is that despite its unattractive appearance, the physical, social, and psychological needs of a small section of America's urban population are met—at least to some extent—in such places. Until we know more about the services that skid row performs in the total pattern of urban life, most attempts to abolish it will be doomed to disappointment.

The term, skid row, appears to have originated in Seattle at the turn of the century. Yessler Street, which sloped to Puget Sound, was greased and logs were skidded down into the water. Along this "skid road" were many taverns, amusement places, and hotels frequented by the men who came to Seattle during the log-shipping season. Yessler Street has formed the prototype of skid rows which include New York's famed Bowery, Chicago's West Madison Street, St. Louis' Chestnut and Market Streets, and similar areas in Copenhagen, Helsinki, Amsterdam, and Paris.

Skid row is usually located near the city's central business district in what the urban sociologist calls the "zone of transition." It is an area characterized by severe physical deterioration—most of the commercial establishments and dwellings are substandard. Hotels and "flophouses," inexpensive restaurants, pawn shops and clothing stores, religious mission, men's service centers, and bars are the usual establishments in the area.

The stereotype of the homeless man in the 1920s was the "hobo." During the depression of the 1930s homelessness and wandering were far from uncommon and, indeed were the normal condition for a sizeable portion of the poor.

Since then the skid row population has declined in number, and many of the Ancient Mariners of the rails and roads have settled down. Although still almost entirely male, it is no longer the mobile group it used to be when the hobo was a familiar sight on the American landscape. A large proportion of the men are now permanent residents living impoverished, homeless lives in numerous missions, cheap hotels, and flophouses, and working when they can as casual laborers.

Though Donald J. Bogue in his study of Chicago's skid row found that the majority of the men could not be defined as alcoholics or even excessive drinkers, the incidence of "problem drinkers" is high in skid row.

The hard core of alcoholism offenders today is found in the 10 to 15 percent of the alcoholic population residing on skid row. They compose the largest portion of the more than one million arrests made annually in the United States on charges of public drunkenness. A great number of these are the repeated arrests of the same men. These chronic drunks are arrested, convicted, sentenced, jailed, and released—only to be rearrested, often within hours or days. They are the men from skid row for whom the door of the jail is truly a "revolving door."

Information gathered by the author and C. Wayne Gordon showed that the usual habitat of the chronic drunkenness offender, when not in jail, is skid row. Of 187 men interviewed in a county jail, we found that each had been sentenced at least twice on a charge of public intoxication. A closer look at these men may give insight into some of the causes and functions of a skid row.

The chronic drunkenness offenders average 48 years old; they are older on the average, therefore than all other groups of law offenders, all other groups of alcoholics, and American males in general.

Those most frequently represented are of English and Irish descent. The Irish made up 35 percent of the sample, and their proportion is even higher among the older men. Though Italians made up a significant part of this county's population, they were only 2 percent of the sample of drunken offenders.

Forty-one percent of these men had never married./Of those who had married, 96 percent had been separated, divorced, or widowed. Practically all of them had either failed to establish families or those they had established had broken down. Only 2 percent were living with their wives at the time of arrest. (In the county studied, only 11 percent of men in the same age brackets had broken marriages.)

Seventy percent had not gone beyond grade school, compared to 40 percent in the county at large. Sixty-eight percent were unskilled workers, 22 percent skilled, and only 3 percent professional, compared to 13, 46 and 22 percent in the general population.

Thirty-nine percent came from families broken before the future derelicts were fifteen years old—an extremely high percentage. The relationships they did have with their parents were very poor—they were seriously deprived emotionally, socially, and psychologically. Tested and rated on a scale designed to show the degree of adolescent adjustment, 86 percent were rated poor, and only 10 percent were "adequate or average."

The skid-row alcoholic drinks to be able to adjust to a life which is harsh, insecure, unrewarding, without dignity. The pattern and the need are set early. There are, however, other possible patterns of adjustment.

Using the age at which a man was committed for a second public drunkness offense as a breakpoint, the group of men studied fall into two types described here as the "early skid" and the "late skid" careers.

The early skid pattern includes about half of the offenders. Two-fifths had been jailed twice in their twenties, and the others by their early thirties. The early skid pattern represents serious social maladjustment in youth carrying over into middle adulthood: poor work records outside of institutions; poor marital adjustment, if any.

The late skid men did not experience their second drunk conviction until in their forties or even fifties. During the time they were developing dependence upon alcohol, they often had stable jobs and families for long periods. Apparent in the late skid career is physical decline and great difficulty in maintaining economic stability in physically taxing marginal jobs. Younger men replace the late skid on the casual daylaborer jobs. His drinking increases, and finally his tolerance for alcohol declines.

The early skid drinks because of early social or psychiatric crippling, the late skid because of decline and failure as he approaches old age.

The skid row alcoholic is and perhaps has always been at the bottom of the socioeconomic ladder—he is isolated, uprooted, unattached, disorganized, demoralized, and homeless. In this predicament he drinks to excess. Admittedly through his own behavior, he is the least respected member of the community, and his treatment by the community has been at best negative and expedient.

In fairness it should be pointed out that in the last four years certain pioneer rehabilitation efforts have been started. Half-Way Houses bridge the gap between skid row living, on the one hand, and independent existence in the community, on the other. The Volunteers of America of Los Angeles are conducting a demonstration project on the rehabilitation of skid row alcoholic men.

On the whole, however, the homeless man has never attained or else has lost the self-esteem and sense of human dignity on which any successful program of treatment and rehabilitation must probably be based. He is caught in a vicious circle: lack or loss of self-esteem produces behavior which in turn causes him to be further discredited publicly, and this further impairs his self-esteem. Any effective therapeutic program would have to break up this cycle.

We still know much too little about the factors causing skid rows and the homeless, uprooted men who inhabit them.

January 1964

How Teachers
Learn to Help Children Fail

ESTELLE FUCHS

Ideally, public schools exist to educate the child. But a
high percentage of pupils fail as early as the fifth or sixth
grade, especially in the urban slums. For many children,
the educational process bogs down at a time when it has
barely begun. Now, educators and social scientists have
proposed a number of theories to explain this high rate of
failure among slum-school children. One of them is that the
slum-school system's tacit belief that social conditions
outside the school make such failures inevitable *does* make
such failures inevitable.

How this expectation of failure affects the instruction
of lower-class children and becomes a self-fulfilling
prophecy is suggested in data collected by Hunter College's Project TRUE (Teacher Resources for Urban Education), a study that focused on the experiences of 14
fledgling teachers in New York's inner-city elementary
schools. As part of the study, several new teachers tape-
recorded accounts of their first-semester teaching experi-

ences in "special service" schools—schools that invariably had high Negro or Puerto Rican enrollments, retarded reading levels among the students, and constant discipline problems.

The following excerpts from one teacher's account show how the slum school gradually instills, in even the best-intentioned teacher, the prevailing rationale for its own failure: The idea that in the slum, it is the child and the family who fail, but never the school.

October 26

Mrs. Jones, the sixth-grade teacher, and I were discussing reading problems. I said, "I wonder about my children. They don't seem too slow; they seem average. Some of them even seem to be above average. I can't understand how they can grow up to be fifth-and sixth-graders and still be reading on the second-grade level. It seems absolutely amazing."

Mrs. Jones [an experienced teacher] explained about the environmental problems that these children have. "Some of them never see a newspaper. Some of them have never been on the subway. The parents are so busy having parties and things that they have no time for their children. They can't even take them to a museum or anything. It's very important that the teacher stress books."

Mrs. Jones tells her class, "If anyone asks you what you want for Christmas, you can say you want a book." She told me that she had a 6-1 class last year, and it was absolutely amazing how many children had never even seen a newspaper. They can't read Spanish either. So she said that the educational problem lies with the parents. They are the ones that have to be educated.

It's just a shame that the children suffer. This problem will take an awful lot to straighten it out. I guess it won't take one day or even a year; it will take time.

December 14

Here I am, a first-grade teacher. I get a great thrill out of these children being able to read but I often wonder, "Am I teaching them how to read or are they just stringing along sight words that they know?" I never had a course in college for teaching phonetics to children. In this school we have had conferences about it, but I really wish that one of the reading teachers would come in and specifically show me how to go about teaching phonetics. I have never gotten a course like this and it is a difficult thing, especially when there is a language barrier and words are quite strange to these children who can't speak English. How can they read English? We have a great responsibility on our shoulders and teachers should take these things seriously.

January 4

Something very, very important and different has happened to me in my school. It all happened the last week before the vacation on Tuesday. Mr. Frost, our principal, came over to me and asked if I would be willing to take over a second-grade class starting after the vacation. Well, I looked at him and I said, "Why?"

He told me briefly that the registers in the school have dropped and according to the board of education the school must lose a teacher. Apparently he was getting rid of a second-grade teacher and he wanted to combine two of the first-grade classes. The registers on the first grade were the lowest in the school, I believe. Anyway, he told me that he was going to all the afternoon first-grade teachers asking if any of them would be willing to change in the middle of the term. He said he thought perhaps someone would really want it and, instead of his just delegating a person, it would be better if he asked each one individually.

I was torn between many factors. I enjoyed my class very, very much and I enjoyed teaching the first grade. But because I was teaching afternoon session (our school runs on two different sessions), I was left out of many of the goings-on within the school as my hours were different and it also sort of conflicted with my home responsibilities. Well, with these two points in mind, I really felt that I would rather stay with my class than to switch over in the middle of the term.

But he explained further that some of the classes would not remain the same because there would be many changes made. So, being the type of person that I am, I felt that, even though I did want to stay with my class and the children and the first grade, if something had to be done in the school, there was no way of stopping it and I might as well do it. I explained to Mr. Frost that even though I wouldn't want to change in the middle—after all it would be a whole new experience, two classes of children would be suffering by the change—but if it had to be done I would be willing to take on the new responsibility.

With that, Mr. Frost said, "Thank you," and said he would go around to the other teachers to see if anyone really wanted to change. Well, already I felt that it was going to be me, but I wasn't sure.

A little later on in the day I was taking my class to recess, and we were lining up in the hall. I spoke to Miss Lane, another teacher, and she said that he had also spoken to her. At that point Mr. Frost came over and told me that he was sorry but that I had been the one elected. Well, I said that I hoped that I would be able to do a good job, and that was that.

From that point on, there was an awful lot of talk in the school. Everybody was talking about it, at least, everyone who knew something about the matter. So all the afternoon first-grade teachers and all the morning first-grade teachers knew, and many of the new teachers (those that I came into the school with), and apparently there was a lot of business going on that I can't begin to describe because I don't know how the whole thing started in the first place. However, from the office I did find out that it wasn't Mr. Frost's fault or anything that the second-grade teacher was going to be dismissed. It was a directive from higher up that stated he would lose a teacher. How he chose this particular teacher to let go I really can't say. I understand that they really didn't get along too well and neither of them were too happy in the school working together.

Everything went so quickly and everybody was talking to me. Mrs. Parsons spoke to me. She is my assistant principal. She was supervisor of the first grade and she will be in charge of the second grade also. I was told that I would have to take over the new class on January 2, the first day that we return from the vacation. I really felt terrible about my children, but it was something that had to be done and I did it.

Thursday, Mr. Frost talked to the other afternoon teachers and myself. He referred to me as the hero and he said, "Now it is your turn to be heroes also." He asked the afternoon first-grade teachers if they would be willing to have their registers become higher by having my 27 children split up among the four remaining afternoon classes, or did they think he should have them split up among all the first-grade classes, some of which met in the morning.

He was straightforward, saying that he didn't think it would be a good idea for the children to be split up among all the first-grade teachers. I agreed with him. He felt that it would be trying on the parents and on the children to have a whole new schedule worked out. After all, if you're used to going to school from 12 to 4, coming to school from 7:30 to 12 is quite a difference. It would be very, very hard on the parents. Especially in this neighborhood where sometimes they have a few children in the same grade, a few in different grades. So I agreed with Mr. Frost. The other teachers didn't seem to happy about the idea, but they said they would go along with it.

Mr. Frost and Mrs. Parsons worked out a plan whereby the 1-1 class register would go up to 35 which is generally what a 1-1 class has. The 1-3 class register would go up to 32 or 33. And so forth down the line. 1-5 (my class) would be erased. The teachers didn't think it was so bad then, but we all did have added responsibilities.

Mr. Frost then added that if we had any children in our classes that we felt did not belong, this was our chance to have them changed, since there would be many interclass transfers in order to make more homogeneous classes. So we all had to sit down and think—"Who belongs? Who doesn't belong?" I, of course, had to decide where 27 children would belong.

I went through my class and divided them into groups to the best of my ability. In the 1-1 class, I put Joseph R., who scored the highest on the reading-readiness test. As a result of his score and his work in class, I felt Joseph did belong in the 1-1 class. Lydia A., who I believe is a very smart girl and who wasn't really working as well as she could in my class, I felt belonged in the 1-1 class. Lydia scored second highest on the reading-readiness test. In the 1-1 class, I also put Anita R. Anita is a bit older than the rest of the children but she has caught on most beautifully to most phases of school work even though she just came to the United States last March. Also, she scored the same as Lydia on the reading-readiness test.

Then I decided that I would put Robert M. in the 1-1 class. I felt strongly that Robert was by far the best child in my class. Robert did every bit of the work ever assigned. He caught on very, very quickly to all phases of work besides doing his work well, quickly, efficiently, and neatly. Even though on reading-readiness he only scored in the 50th percentile, I felt he really stood out and I also felt that once you're in a "1" class, unless you really don't belong, you have a better chance. The "1" class is really the only class that you would term a "good" class. So those four children I recommended for the 1-1 class.

Then I went down the line and for the 1-3 class, I picked nine children, really good children who, on the whole, listened and did their work. Most of them scored in the 50th and 40th percentile on reading-readiness, and they were coping with school problems very, very well. In the 1-7 class, I put the slower children and in the 1-9 class, of course, which is Mrs. Gould's, I put all the children that really weren't doing well in school work at all. First, Alberto S. Alberto is still not able to write his name. Then I put Beatrice L., Stella S., Pedro D., and several others, who really were not working well, in the 1-9 class.

I know that the other teachers do have a big job before them because whichever class these children are placed in will not have been doing exactly the same work. The children either have much to catch up on or they might review some of the work, and the teachers will have to be patient either way. I really don't think anyone will have serious discipline problems, except perhaps in the 1-1 class where Lydia and Anita have been placed.

The time came when I had to tell the children that I would not be their teacher anymore. Well, as young as they are, I think that many of them caught on immediately, and before I could say anything, faces were very, very long and the children were mumbling, "But I wanted you for a teacher."

That was all I needed! I felt even worse than I felt when I found out that I wouldn't be with them anymore. So I continued talking and I told them that it's just something that happens and that I would still be in the school and maybe next year they would get me when they go to the second grade. I told them that I would miss them all, that they would have a lot of fun in their new classes, and they would learn a lot. And, of course, I said, "You know all the other teachers. Some of you will get Mrs. Lewis. Some will get Miss Lane, some will get Miss Taylor, and some will get Mrs. Gould."

To my astonishment Anita kept saying over and over, "But I want you for a teacher. But I want you for a teacher."

I looked around the room. Most of the children were sitting there with very, very long faces. Joseph C. was sitting there with the longest face you could imagine, Robert G. said he didn't want another teacher, and all of a sudden Joseph started crying and just didn't stop. He cried all the way out into the hall when we got dressed to go home. I spoke to him softly and said, "Joseph, wouldn't you like Miss Lane for a teacher?" She was standing right near me, and finally he stopped crying.

I said goodbye to them and that I would see them all. And that was the end of my class. . . .

Good schools. Poor schools. What is a good school? Is a good school one that is in a good neighborhood, that has middle-class children? Is a poor school one in a depressed area where you have Negro and Puerto Rican children? These are common terms that people refer to all the time. They hear your school is on Wolf Street—"Oh, you must be in a bad school."

I don't really think that that is what a good or a bad school is. I think a good school is a school that is well run, has a good administration, has people that work together well, has good discipline and where the children are able to learn and also, of course, where there are numerous facilities for the children and the teachers. In my estimation a poor or a bad school would be one in which the administration and the teachers do not work together, are not working in the best interests of the children, and where learning is not going on. Also, a poor school is one where you don't have proper facilities. I am not acquainted with many of the public schools, and I really can't say that the ones that I know are better or worse.

I believe my school is a pretty good school. It isn't in the best neighborhood. There are many, many problems in my school but on the whole I think that the teachers and the administration work together and I do believe that they are doing the best they can with the problems that are around.

You have to remember that in a school such as ours the children are not as ready and willing to learn as in schools in the middle-class neighborhoods.

When a new teacher enters the classroom, she must learn the behavior, attitudes, and skills required in the new situation. Much of this learning is conscious. Some of it is not. What is significant is that, while on the job, the teacher is socialized to her new role—she is integrated into the society of the school, and learns the values, beliefs and attitudes that govern its functioning.

The saga of class 1-5 shows the subtle ways in which one new teacher is socialized to her job. In just a few months, she accepts the demands of the school organization and its prevailing rationale for student failure.

The new teacher of class 1-5 in a slum school begins her career with a warm, friendly attitude toward her students. She respects and admires their abilities and is troubled by what the future holds for them: By the sixth grade in her school, educational failure is very common.

Very early in her teaching career, however, a more experienced teacher exposes this new teacher to the belief, widely held, that the children come from inferior backgrounds and that the deficits in their homes—expressed here as lack of newspapers and parental care—prevent educational achievement. That the teachers and the school as an institution contribute to the failure of the children is never even considered as a possible cause. The beginning teacher, in her description of what happens to class 1-5, then provides us with a graphic account of the ways in which this attitude can promote failure.

First, let us examine the actual instruction of the children. Early in her career, this new, very sincere teacher is painfully aware of her own deficiencies. Unsure about her teaching of so fundamental a subject as reading, she raises serious questions about her own effectiveness. As yet, she has not unconsciously accepted the notion that the failure of children stems from gaps in their backgrounds. Although no consensus exists about reading methodology, the teacher tells us that there are serious weaknesses in feedback evaluation—and that she is unable to find out what the children have been taught or what they have really learned.

By the end of the term, all this has changed. By that time, the eventual failure of most of class 1-5 has been virtually assured. And the teacher has come to rationalize this failure in terms of pupil inadequacy.

In the particular case of class 1-5, the cycle of failure begins with a drop in the number of students registered in the school. The principal loses a teacher, which in turn means dissolving a class and subsequently distributing its children among other classes. The principal and the teachers have no control over this event. In the inner-city schools, education budgets, tables of organization, and directions from headquarters create conditions beyond the control of the administrators and teachers who are in closest touch with the children.

A drop in pupil registers would seemingly provide the opportunity for a higher adult-pupil ratio and, consequently, more individualized instruction and pedagogical supports for both youngsters and teachers. In a suburban school, this is probably what would have occurred. But in this slum school, the register drop leads to the loss of a teacher, larger classes, and—perhaps most important—increased time spent by the administrator and his staff on the mechanics of administration rather than on the supervision of instruction. (Why *this* particular teacher is released is unclear, though her substitute status and low rank in the staff hierarchy probably contribute to her release.) As a result many classes are disrupted, several first-grade class registers grow larger, time for instruction is lost, and concern is felt by teachers and pupils alike.

An even more significant clue to the possible eventual failure of the children is described in poignant detail—when the teacher tells how the youngsters in her class are to be distributed among the other first-grade classes. Educators now know that children mature at different rates; that they have different rates of learning readiness; and the developmental differences between boys and girls are relevant to learning. To forecast the educational outcome of youngsters at this early stage of their development, without due provision for these normal growth variations, is a travesty of the educational process. Yet here, in the first half of the first grade, a relatively inexperienced young teacher, herself keenly aware of her own deficiencies as an educator, is placed in the position of literally deciding the educational future of her charges.

A few are selected for success—"I felt that once you're in a '1' class, unless you really don't belong, you have a better chance. The '1' class is really the only class that you would term a 'good' class." Several children are placed in a class labeled "slow." And the remaining youngsters are relegated to a state of limbo, a middle range that does not carry the hope of providing a "better chance."

Thus, before these youngsters have completed a full four months of schooling, their educational futures have been "tracked": All through the grades, the labels of their class placement will follow them, accompanied by teacher attitudes about their abilities. Some youngsters are selected very early for success, others written off as slow. Because differential teaching occurs and helps to widen the gap between children, the opportunity to move from one category to another is limited. In addition, the children too become aware of the labels placed upon them. And their pattern for achievement in later years is influenced by their feelings of success of failure in early school experiences.

The teacher, as she reflects upon what a "good" or a "bad" school is, continues to include how well the children learn as a significant criterion, together with good relations between staff and administration. But the children in her school do not achieve very well academically, so when describing her school as "good," she stresses the good relations between the administration and the teachers. The fact that the children do not learn does not seem so important now: "the children are not as ready and willing to learn as in schools in middle-class neighborhoods."

How well our teacher has internalized the attitude that deficits of the children themselves explain their failure in school! How normal she now considers the administrative upheavals and their effects upon teachers and children! How perfectly ordinary she considers the "tracking" of youngsters so early in their school years!

The teacher of class 1-5 has been socialized by the school to accept its structure and values. Despite her sincerity and warmth and obvious concern for the children, this teacher is not likely to change the forecast of failure for most of these children—because she has come to accept the very structural and attitudinal factors that make failure nearly certain. In addition, with all her good intentions, she has come to operate as an agent determining the life chances of the children in her class—by distributing them among the ranked classes on the grade.

This teacher came to her job with very positive impulses. She thought highly of her youngsters and was disturbed that, with what appeared to be good potential, there was so much failure in the school in the upper grades. She looked inward for ways in which she might improve her efforts to forestall retardation. She was not repelled by the neighborhood in which she worked. There is every indication that she had the potential to become a very effective teacher of disadvantaged youngsters.

Her good impulses, however, were not enough. This young teacher, unarmed with the strength that understanding the social processes involved might have given her and having little power within the school hierarchy, was socialized by the attitudes of those around her, by the administration, and by the availability of a suitable rationale to explain her and the school's failure to fulfill their ideal roles. As a result she came to accept traditional slum-school attitudes toward the children—and traditional attitudes toward school organization as the way things have to be. This teacher is a pleasant, flexible, cooperative young woman to have on one's staff. But she has learned to behave and think in a way that perpetuates a process by which disadvantaged children continue to be disadvantaged.

The organizational structure of the large inner-city school and the attitudes of the administrators and teachers within it clearly affect the development of the children attending. No theory proposed to explain the academic failure of poor and minority-group children can ignore the impact of the actual school experience and the context in which it occurs.

September 1968

Becky and the Telegraph Avenue Scene

MARC PILISUK/LILYAN BINDER/CLAIRE BRADY
SANDRA BROEMEL/ROBERT HART/ANN OHREN
WILLIAM SMOLAK/SUSAN CADY

In the past ten years, increasing numbers of young people have become alienated from the mainstream of American values. They have expressed their alienation overtly through civil rights sit-ins, antiwar demonstrations, ghetto riots, and most recently through massive participation in what the press has called campus disorders. On a more individual level they have gone through a developing process of first speaking out, then acting out, and then, for many, dropping out.

This dropping out phenomenon takes different forms for different people. For some it means dropping out of college or even high school for a year to think things over and "get it together." For others, it means leaving a well-paying establishment job and splitting to the country to "live off the land." For younger adolescents it may mean going on the road to gain freedom from family and home town to travel and to meet new, hopefully "better," people.

Most people seem to hope that dropping out will mean

living a less structured life with fewer planned activities and more time to think, hang around, take dope and spend time with friends. Many realize that there are certain risks involved in dropping out from society—that there will be less assurance of where the next meal will come from and that their life style will make them more vulnerable to police busts for drugs, hitchhiking, loitering and a variety of other charges. They are willing to take these risks, however, in order to escape what they view as the phony values of "the establishment."

The young people who come to Telegraph Avenue in Berkeley, California, are in many ways typical of this whole generation of young dropouts. On another level, however, they provide perhaps the most extreme example of the counterculture that is now developing in America. They are living in a city that has shown itself to be capable of both sustained political protest and sustained political repression. They are attempting to create their counter love culture in the teeth of an escalating situation calculated to squelch both cultural and political dissent. They feel themselves to be the daily victims of police harassment. They know that the drugs that many of them are taking are conducive to social withdrawal and paranoia rather than openness and interpersonal sharing. Yet, in the face of what they view to be a deteriorating situation on the Avenue, many of them persist in believing that there have been times in the recent past when the flower culture has actually thrived and that love and some type of cultural, spiritual or political revolution could once again make this counterculture a living reality for all who want to participate in it.

Since ideal and reality sometimes diverge, it is important to examine what such communities of middle-class dropouts actually offer to the young people who come to a place like Berkeley's Telegraph Avenue. Rejecting the material motives of mainstream culture, how do they manage to survive in a subculture denigrated by the larger community and constricted by poverty?

In an effort to provide answers to such questions as these, we undertook an ethnographic study of life on the Avenue beginning with the Telegraph Avenue-South Campus area, its various coffee houses, hangouts, sidewalk art displays and the Free Clinic. As trust developed, members of the team were able to interview a number of informants in their houses or at convenient hangouts on the Avenue. The interviews frequently went into great depth in matters of personal concern and many relationships with interviewees continued over a period of several months. Most interviews, (with the obvious exception of group interviews with a special "continuation class" of Berkeley High ex-dropouts) were individual and our informants proved to be remarkably candid. Becky was one of these informants. Becky had slightly more money (and more overt concern about money) than most of our other informants, but her case provides a glimpse of what the dropout scene is like.

Becky was seen by the interviewer on three occasions between November 1969 and January 1970. The first two interviews were in Becky's home and lasted about two hours each. The third interview, lasting about an hour, began at Becky's home. At Becky's suggestion, she and the interviewer then drove to Telegraph Avenue, walked around for awhile, then went to the Heidelberg Restaurant for some coffee and dessert.

Becky was introduced to the interviewer through another member of the research team, a girl who had once been Becky's roommate. The interviewer found Becky quite willing to be interviewed, well informed as to what was happening on the Avenue, and quite articulate, making her one of our most helpful contacts.

Identifying Data: Becky was a 23 year old articulate Caucasian girl who had been living on or near Telegraph Ave-

closing of Pepe's Pizza had greatly affected the street people in that Pepe's was "the major center of dealing and of just sitting around to socialize with friends." Evidently, it was felt that Tiajuana Taco, which has just recently opened, would take the place of Pepe's, but the owners of Tiajuana Taco passed a new rule that people could not sit around inside unless the were eating something. Standing in front has also been discouraged. Becky seemed unhappy about this and felt that this was something planned in conjunction with the police.

As winter approached, Becky saw fewer people on the street. She hypothesized that as the weather got colder, people on the Avenue were no longer able to sleep on roof tops and in doorways. They were either leaving town or finding better places to stay. Another result of the cool weather was that a new meeting place had become the basement of the First Baptist Church which remained open until midnight. People went there to shoot pool, play cards and checkers, watch TV and to socialize.

Becky knew of no one who is really a "street person" who lives in the Bay Area. A street person, according to Becky, was one who literally "lives on the street and makes his living there." They are there every day, not just on weekends. Most are from out of the Bay Area. "No one really knows where they go when they leave Berkeley, but there are always rumors of a groovy place to go—like Monterey or the latest, Stockton." Sometimes people come back after a few weeks or months. Most agreed that Berkeley was a hot spot because of the police but that generally one could "do his own thing" here.

Becky had some mixed feelings about crash pads. While on the one hand they were free, on the other hand, she felt that "a girl crashing in some guy's pad was expected to sleep with one of the guys there." She said that "when you feel like it—maybe you're glad to—but sometimes you just want to be alone." Girls resent it.

She said that nearly everyone she knew had had some venereal disease at least once, but that she knows of a few exceptions. "All you have to do if you have it is to go down to the Free Clinic to get cured." But venereal disease was so easy to get again that many were reinfected within a few weeks.

Becky claimed that pregnancy was a common occurrence on the Avenue because most people didn't use any type of contraceptive. She felt that hardly any girls are on the pill because they had to pay for them, wait weeks for an appointment at one of the clinics in the area, and especially because most girls couldn't be bothered with taking them each day, particularly if they were using drugs and tripping out a lot. She knew of no street person who had gotten an abortion because it took money, but she did once know of two students who did. Becky said that many girls have miscarriages and some have their baby. Some babies are taken away because the mothers are unfit to care for them. She wasn't sure whether the State or the parents took the kids away. Some girls give their babies to their parents to care for. (Other informants seemed to look upon the baby as a more permanent tie than could be found elsewhere. Some men just like children and would favor a pregnant girl or one living with a young child).

Drugs: Becky seemed to feel, as do most street people, that marijuana "is a daily staple in the household." She believed that the street people use mainly pot and acid because if you are on harder stuff (especially heroin) you cannot even walk straight and are picked up too easily by the police. "The hard stuff," she claims "is used mainly by the blacks who come in from Oakland or other cities to buy it." Grass and hashish were used more often than acid since "the longer one drops acid the less effect it has." There were diminishing returns as one's body gets used to it. "The first few times on acid," according to Becky, "are the best unless you stay away from it a few months then come back to it." Kids don't think about the bad things acid does to their bodies, but are quite aware of the recent findings. They believe the findings, generally, but don't care and try not to think about it. Almost all people had bad trips now and then and were panicked by the "bad trip" movies they see, but kept taking it anyway. Acid use did seem to be on the decline, however. People tended to stop using acid when they outgrew it or stopped getting any new insights from it. For Becky "acid is more of a 'fun-light-happy-play drug' and grass is more for heavy thought." She did not mention any of the other drugs in use on the Avenue such as speed, smack, red devils and cocaine.

Maintenance: After Becky graduated from college she found a summer job as a waitress and worked almost night and day to save as much money as she could so that she could buy a car and come to California. She was living with her parents during this time. She managed to save about $2,000. She paid $1,000 for a VW camper and $500 for repairs. She left for California in the fall of 1968; however, the camper broke down on the way. She thought the camper was not repairable so she shipped her belongings on to California and hitchhiked the rest of the way. She had $250 left when she reached Berkeley. She found an apartment, and, soon after, a job as a lab technician at a local laboratory at $400 a month. During this time, she took on a second job as a salesgirl for a fabrics store to supplement her income, but she quit the sales job after one week because she had no free time.

One day in April 1969, a friend said that Becky didn't look very happy on her job. She quit her lab technician job the next day. Then she decided to take a $200 course in massage techniques. After taking the course which lasted several weeks, the school hired her to be a masseuse in their office. Even though she was making good money, she quit this job after two months. At the same time she moved out of her apartment because it was costing her too much money. She rented a garage for awhile, then lived in a local commune. In July, she became sick and moved back in with her old roommate again. In mid-August, after being unemployed for about three months, she put an ad in the paper offering her services as a masseuse. The phone rang almost nonstop and she had more calls than she could handle. She used the basement as a studio or went out to the person's home to give a massage. (This practice not uncommonly leads to physical exploitation paid for by a bad check.) In the summer she taught a massage program. A month later she went back to work as a lab technician at the same job she had before. Due to a general shortage of work, however, she was laid off two weeks later. As in past times of unemployment, Becky always felt that she would find another job soon; except this time she had difficulty and began to become depressed. After much discussion, her roommate finally convinced her to apply for unemployment insurance, something that Becky had resisted doing in the past. It was at this point in Becky's life that she was first interviewed for this study. She was living in a large house in which seven people lived, each renting a specific room and sharing the rest. Becky paid $35 a month for the breakfast nook, which she used as her bedroom. She was receiving about $30 a week in unemployment benefits. However, that particular week she had been sick and thus unable to go down to the Employment Department for her check. She had $15 to her name to live on until the next week. She said that, unlike some other street people, "I get anxious when I don't know where my next few meals will come from." She said that now she didn't leave the supermarket without stealing some food. She and others like her would eat fruit and cake off the shelves while walking around the store and then leave empty-handed. For some of the street people taking things from establishment merchants was natural and justifiable. Becky, however, did not like herself at all when she did this, but found it necessary for survival.

During the time she received unemployment benefits, Becky was taking a psysiology course at the University Extension so that she could eventually become a physical therapist. She really enjoyed being a masseuse since she felt that she was good at it and it did a lot to make people feel better. It was important to her to have a job where she did not have to take advantage of people economically. She knew how little money she actually needed to survive and felt that people can live fairly comfortably without charging exorbitant prices for services. She felt that as a physical therapist, "I could help people without taking advantage of them."

Becky saw Bill Miller, a shopkeeper on the Avenue, as an example of someone who made only enough to live himself and did not try to take advantage of people. He not only sold things at reasonable prices but also traded things. "He seems truly interested in the street people and pays about $20 a day to keep a barrel full of apples and sometimes cookies in his shop for kids to eat free."

By the time Becky was interviewed the second time, she had found a job as a waitress at a local restaurant. She had been there five days and was surprised that she actually was enjoying working again. It was a chance to be active again, to earn money and to meet nice people. "It was good luck that I got the job since I was just walking by, saw a 'help wanted' sign and went in." Through some misunderstanding, the three girls who were supposed to work that day didn't show up, so she was put to work immediately on a trial basis. She felt that she is a hard worker and thought the boss was pleased with her work. Her boss said that he would pay $1.65 an hour, but implied that those who work harder would get more. She believed in this philosophy, but was not sure he really meant what he said. She described her boss as a nice guy who "butters-up" the people he likes. She said she could see right through this, but "I butter him up in return because it's fun and people get along better that way." She also liked the other girls and enjoyed the feeling of teamwork.

Five weeks later, when Becky was interviewed for the third time, she reported that she had just gotten fired from her job due to interpersonal problems with her boss. She was vague about what happened but implied that she had gotten romantically involved with her boss and that he became jealous when she later became involved with someone else. She planned to go down to the Employment Department the following week to collect unemployment benefits. After that ran out, she planned to look for some part-time job. She felt that she could never hold a 40 hour a week job. She had no idea what kind of job she would look for, but anything would be fine as long as she could be somewhat independent. It was important to her that she like the people on the job and that they didn't "hassle" her.

Becky explained how people actually living off the street supported themselves. Their money comes mainly from dealing in drugs, panhandling or, for a few, from welfare and unemployment insurance. Generally, the older kids (especially if they have had some college or are politically aware) are more apt to apply for welfare and unemployment. "Kids also live by stealing food or living off others in crash pads."

Becky felt that those who sell their arts and crafts in front of Cody's Bookstore do quite well. They generally sell to outsiders and visitors to the Avenue, since the street people have no money for such things. Becky criticized the fact that nowadays anything homemade will sell as "art". It is the latest fad.

People with no money sleep in some of the large new apartment buildings. They have TV lobbys or roofs where people can sleep if not too obvious. The Berkeley Inn also has a TV room where people can sleep. Sometimes it is packed wall to wall, depending on which clerk is on duty. When it's warm, some people sleep on steps and porches along the Avenue. "People live from day to day. They have poor health because they can't wash often or eat properly." Physical health problems are often let go until they become unbearable. They then go to the Free Clinic where they must wait in line for hours. It is frustrating because after all that waiting, they may just give you a blood test and tell you to come back the next day.

Feelings About the Police: Becky felt that the police park in the lot behind the Berkeley Inn and are dispatched from there. They try to change their tactics all the time, but the people feel they are predictable and not very clever, except for some plainclothes officers.

Plainclothes officers are easily spotted by the big-time drug dealers or by those on the Avenue for a long time. "Generally you learn their faces after a police bust," but they are changed quite often so one must be constantly on guard. "One guy really surprised everyone. He was a black guy with a big natural and a head band. No one suspected." Plainclothes women are around too. They usually wear skirts and carry the kind of purses in which an easily accesible gun can be concealed. Thus, flap-over purses are suspect. One plainclothes woman had short blond hair and looked like a PE teacher. "Harry, the public relations officer with the friendly manner . . . informs to other police who eventually get you in the end. He is 'two-faced' and not to be trusted."

In December Becky felt that the end-of-the-summer push

to clean up the Avenue was still on. Many people were still being arrested just for loitering or for not having an I.D. on them. These people were taken down to jail, and, since they had no money for bail, were kept as long as legally possible. Thus, they were released just before the legal deadline (72 hours) at which time a legal hearing must be held. In this way, the kids were cleared off the streets over the weekends. Becky felt that these types of actions were worse at the end of summer in an attempt "to get kids to leave the area," even though many kids leave the area anyway at the end of the summer to return to school.

Plans for the Future: At the time that Becky was last interviewed, she seemed to be going through a period of self-improvement. She said she wanted to drop all things and "people who are dragging me down." She did not elaborate, but clearly was in a period when she wanted to do things her own way—privately, independently and on her own timetable. It was as if she were searching for something within herself and examining what she really wanted. She said she was reading more lately and going on outings to the country alone. She said she had been staying off the Avenue generally, except to go to the Mediterranean occasionally for coffee. She preferred the Mediterranean to the Forum because the people at the "Med" are older and more "together." She was trying to leave the past behind and pull herself up. As she put it, she had wasted a lot of time and was now trying to "make up for lost time." She said, "Maybe I can't, though. I have my ups and downs as before, but I'm more hang loose now. I know I can fall pretty low and still survive and exist. It isn't fun, but you're still alive. So now that I've been there I'm not as uptight about falling a little. I can be more flexible. The ups and downs are still here, but now I'm aiming up."

The last report heard from Becky was that in March she

had saved $450 working again for a brief time as a masseuse and was planning to leave Berkeley for Mexico.

Our informants generally left home to escape an unfulfilling or unbearable family situation and to find themselves in a larger world. Their parents and their parents' community were stifling and unsupportive. Their parents especially seemed to lack understanding of their difficulties and, in the majority of cases, could not risk trying to understand. Instead, the parents attempted to force their values on their offspring, while their behavior as adults strongly indicated the failure of these values to provide confirmation of their worth as adequate models for the young. Becky's case was somewhat unusual in that her parents showed more than customary concern and effort to keep in communication with their daughter.

The drug experience, expecially the psychedelics, in some instances accentuated the disaffection and distance the adolescent felt from his parents and his community. This experience increased his need to get to a place where there were other young people with whom he might share his new view of life. The influence of drugs must be seen as increasing (often in a few hours!) the already wide gap in the communication and understanding existing between parent and child in our society. Many young people are not joining the alcoholic brotherhood of their parents. They are exchanging this ritual for rituals of their own. This rejection of alcohol as a socializer also acted to create distance and ill will between parent and child. The differences at home, combined with the absence of a feeling of connection with the community, and a glorified awareness of the world outside their home town as provided by the media, led many of our informants to break with their families and head out on their own.

Young people of this generation, more than any other, have the resources available to them to leave home and get far enough away to feel independent. Some of our informants left home with hundreds of dollars. Despite these circumstances, it is questionable whether so many would have left home had there not been a mecca like California, and the San Francisco Bay Area in particular, to gravitate to. If there had been no place to pin their hopes on, could they have left home at all? So, in varying stages of initiation into the hip subculture, young people converged on the Bay Area in the middle and late 1960s. They came to the area sharing three important characteristics: 1) disenchantment with their parents and their community as models, 2) enough emotional and financial resources to make a break with those models, and 3) a desire to find values and life styles they could relate to and a community that they could accept and that would accept them as first class members.

Nearly all our informants asserted that the climate for such a new community was in evidence in Berkeley in 1965 and 1966. The psychedelic drug culture, already past its peak in San Francisco, was blooming in Berkeley. But, as in San Francisco, this flowering was short lived. Many hip people in Berkeley seemed to sense the decline of the Avenue scene and were already, in 1966, heading for such places as Big Sur, Mendocino, and New Mexico. The population on the Avenue became younger each year. There was less good will between the street people and the official community surrounding the Avenue. The police presence on the Avenue, in the form of harassment and drug arrests, was felt more intensely. Unadulterated psychedelic drugs became harder to find. There was, at this time, an influx of "harder" drugs, especially methedrine and heroin. The hangouts of the Avenue people were, one by one, shut down due to increased city government pressure.

Despite these changes, young people continued to flood

to the Avenue hoping they would find something there that they could not find at home, whether home was Kansas or the Berkeley Hills. By the time of our interviews, the Avenue itself was for most of our informants, all of whom have known the Avenue over a period of years, a place to walk through as quickly as possible. At most, it was a place to meet a friend and move on to more comfortable surroundings such as someone's home in the area.

Consider, then, a young person coming to Telegraph Avenue in, say, 1968 in search of a supportive community in which he could relax, try on a variety of values, share his growing pains with other young people, and look for new models to help him nurture his as yet undeveloped self-image. What he found was something quite different. He found that what he had in common with his fellow travelers, what commonly occupied much of his and their time, was the hassle to survive in a larger community that was far from supportive. He had to toughen himself up quickly and learn the ropes of living on the street without resources. He had to do this without the reassurances of friendly smiles from the adult world who probably would approve in theory of a teenager's quest for life and adventure but would certainly not approve of his style of going after it. He had to grow without the guidance of his older "spiritual" brothers (who would have respected his complete defection from middle-class norms and values) because those older brothers had either left Berkeley for greener fields or stayed in their quiet Berkeley homes making increasingly rare contact with the Avenue. Without the support of any sizeable or powerful segment of the more stable adult world, he was forced to grow up fast—faster than he wanted to, or, in fact, was able to comfortably. He was, then, forced to maintain himself on the fringes of the wider society—panhandling, dealing drugs, at times stealing from his peers, sharing his goods more from absolute necessity than from a feeling of brotherhood, getting welfare assistance if he was able to and if he could reconcile himself to receiving aid in this way. His sleeping arrangements ("crashing"), often in a different place every night, were equally incongruent with his manifest reasons for coming to Berkeley—to "get his head together," to gain enough insight and understanding of himself and his environment and to be able to act as a unit in going after what he wanted from life.

In the same way, without a stable frame of reference (home or community) to work from, his relationships with his peers in general and with the opposite sex were even more ephemeral than might be expected of someone his age. We came to feel that, in this regard, the "here-and-now" philosophy advocated by many of our informants was in part a defense against the full blown awareness of the difficulty of establishing enduring relationships. At the same time, though, we found that often in our discussions of the behavior of our population we were overlooking its young age. Since our informants were living in the adult world, we easily forgot that many of them were teenagers and that even those who were out of their teens were perhaps not prepared to cope with the problems of living and development which they faced daily. We rediscovered that it is characteristic of our culture to keep its young dependent and then, at a certain age, to throw them out into the world to "make it" on their own. We often reflected on the difficulty of being a young person today and expressed relief that we were not in his place.

So, our young person, having been in Berkeley two years, had made many compromises in the name of survival. Of course, we would not expect things to be as he had hoped when he left his parent's home for Berkeley, but now that he has seen what the community had to offer, why didn't he leave? He had discovered that he was not really wanted here, that little was being done to accomodate him and his brothers. He had found little of the guidance or the community he came in search of. He had discovered that not all drug trips are beautiful, that, in fact, when taken when one felt as shakey as he often did, even unadulterated psychedelics could literally blow his mind. Sometimes it took days or weeks to put the pieces back together. He had discovered that some drugs destroyed your brain or were addictive. He had been made aware that almost no one of his brothers, often including himself, could be trusted completely. He had been shown that the police, whom he might have steered clear of in his home town, were "here and now" a constant threat to his freedom. He had learned from bitter experience the hardships of rejecting material values where they were held most reverently—in the city.

Yet, he and his brothers who encompass a wide variety of backgrounds and ages, hold just as reverently to their repudiation of middle-class norms and institutions. And many of them *stay* in Berkeley. We have determined that some are stuck here, not having the resources to make a move. Some like it here, some simply have never given leaving a thought. Some are in the process of getting out into the country or into communes where more and more young people are attempting to find some satisfaction. Finally, there are some, especially those from big eastern cities, who are still really "city people" and Berkeley is the last city, paradise or no, where they feel at all comfortable. Many, then, are here surrounded by, and part of, a community which is perhaps more acutely aware of the ills of the society than any in the country. This awareness, together with a sincere desire to see man grow in a positive direction, is reflected in the basic tenets of their way of life. These tenets are manifestly liberating yet contain an underlying current of despair: "Let everyone do his own thing as long as he harms no one by doing it . . . " is ostensibly a statement of nonjudgmental acceptance. And indeed, that spirit has been and continues to be somewhat in evidence on the Avenue. However, just below the skin of that statement are these tacit additions— " . . . it doesn't make any difference *to me*" and " . . . it doesn't make any difference in the world no matter what you do." The former implies an apathetic isolation from their brothers, the latter an awareness of the near impossibility of diverting the course the larger society is set on.

In the same way, the "live in the here and now" philosophy which our informants invoked and largely adhere to is ostensibly aimed at by choice. The street person does not want to follow in his parent's footsteps. To him, experience is not something you can save up for; awareness does not come with a price tag on it; preoccupation with the future and its security equals denial and fear of the pleasure of the "now." In actuality the young Avenue person does not see living for the future as realistic, much less desirable. Rather, the sentiment seems to be—"live in the now because there may be no *tomorrow*." Unlike his parent's generation, the red carpet of a fantasized future does not roll out before him as he matures; nor does it slow down or stop occasionally so that he might inspect its reality. Instead, the future is rolling itself back to meet him head on and *force* him to acknowledge today as the reality he must survive.

Society can offer the Avenue person no constructive alternatives, no support. He knows this. What society does offer is repression of his most urgent needs: to grow and to identify himself. He knows this as well, that his situation is essentially equivalent to that of every American citizen, but being young and sensitive he feels it more intensely and is more vulnerable to its pain than many others might be. His choices are limited, as are theirs, to techniques of survival.

Medical Ghettos

ANSELM L. STRAUSS

In President Johnson's budget message to Congress this year he proposed a quadrupling of federal spending on health care and medical assistance for the poor to $4.2 billion in fiscal 1968:

The 1968 budget maintains the forward thrust of federal programs designed to improve health care in the nation, to combat poverty, and assist the needy. . . . The rise reflects the federal government's role in bringing quality medical care, particularly to aged and indigent persons.

Three years earlier in a special message to Congress the President had prefaced reintroduction of the medicare bill by saying:

We can—and we must—strive now to assure the availability of and accessibility to the best health care for all Americans, regardless of age or geography or economic status. . . . Nowhere are the needs greater than for the 15 million children of families who live in poverty.

Then, after decades of debate and massive professional and political opposition, the medicare program was passed. It promised to lift the poorest of our aged out of the medical ghetto of charity and into private and voluntary hospital care. In addition, legislation for heart disease and cancer centers was quickly enacted. It was said that such facilities would increase life expectancy by five years and bring a 20 percent reduction in heart disease and cancer by 1975.

Is the medical millenium, then, on its way? The president, on the day before sending the 1968 budget to Congress, said: "Medicare is an unqualified success."

"Nevertheless," he added, "there are improvements which can be made and shortcomings which need prompt attention." The message also noted that there might be some obstacles on the high road to health. The rising cost of medical care, President Johnson stated, "requires an expanded and better organized effort by the federal government in research and studies of the organization and delivery of health care." If the President's proposals are adopted, the states will spend $1.9 billion and the federal government $1 billion in a "Partnership for Health" under the Medicaid program.

Considering the costs to the poor—and to the taxpayers —why don't the disadvantaged get better care? In all the lively debate on that matter, it is striking how little attention is paid to the mismatch between the current organization of American medicine and the life styles of the lower class. The major emphasis is always on how the present systems can be a little better supported or a trifle altered to produce better results.

I contend that the poor will never have anything approaching equal care until our present medical organization undergoes profound reform. Nothing in current legislation or planning will accomplish this. My arguments, in brief, are these:

□ The emphasis in all current legislation is on extending and improving a basically sound system of medical organization.

□ This assumes that all those without adequate medical services—especially the poor—can be reached with minor reforms, without radical transformation of the systems of care.

□ This assumption is false. The reason the medical systems have not reached the poor is because they were never designed to do so. The way the poor think and respond, the way they live and operate, has hardly ever (if ever) been considered in the scheduling, paperwork, organization, and mores of clinics, hospitals, and doctors' offices. The life styles of the poor are different; they must be specifically taken into account. Professionals have not been trained and are not now being trained in the special skills and procedures necessary to do this.

□ These faults result in a vicious cycle which drives the poor away from the medical care they need.

□ Major reforms in medical organizations must come, or the current great inequities will continue, and perhaps grow.

I have some recommendations designed specifically to break up that vicious cycle at various points. These recommendations are built directly upon aspects of the life styles of the poor. They do not necessarily require new money or resources, but they do require rearrangement, reorganization, reallocation—the kind of change and reform which are often much harder to attain than new funds or facilities.

In elaborating these arguments, one point must be nailed down first: The poor definitely get second-rate medical care. This is self-evident to anyone who has worked either with them or in public medical facilities; but there is a good deal of folklore to the effect that the very poor share with the very rich the best doctors and services—the poor getting free in the clinics what only the rich can afford to buy.

The documented statistics of the Department of Health, Education, and Welfare tell a very different story. As of 1964, those families with annual incomes under $2,000 average 2.8 visits per person to a physician each year, compared to 3.8 for those above $7,000.(For children during the crucial years under 15, the ratio is 1.6 to 5.7. The poor tend to have larger families; needless to add, their child mortality rate is also higher.) People with higher incomes (and $7,000 per year can hardly be considered wealthy) have a tremendous advantage in the use of medical specialists—27.5 percent see at least one of them annually, compared to about 13 percent of the poor.

Health insurance is supposed to equalize the burden; but here, too, money purchases better care. Hospital or surgical insurance coverage is closely related to family income, ranging from 34 percent among those with family income of less than $2,000 to almost 90 percent for persons in families of $7,000 or more annual income. At the same time, the poor, when hospitalized, are much more apt to have more than one disorder—and more apt to exhaust their coverage before discharge.

Among persons who were hospitalized, insurance paid for some part of the bill for about 40 percent of patients with less than $2,000 family income, for 60 percent of patients with $2,000-$3,999 family income, and for 80 percent of patients with higher income. Insurance paid three-fourths or more of the bill for approximately 27 percent, 44 percent, and 61 percent of these respective income groups. Preliminary data from the 1964 survey year showed, for surgery or delivery bills paid by insurance, an even more marked association of insurance with income.

Similar figures can be marshaled for chronic illness, dental care, and days of work lost.

Strangely enough, however, *cash* difference (money actually spent for care) is not nearly so great. The under $2,000 per year group spent $112 per person per year, those families earning about three times as much as ($4,000-$7,000) paid $119 per person, and those above $7,000, $153. Clearly, the poor not only get poorer health services but less for their money.

As a result, the poor suffer much more chronic illness and many more working days lost—troubles they are peculiarly ill-equipped to endure. Almost 60 percent of the poor have more than one disabling condition compared to about 24 percent of other Americans. Poor men lose 10.2 days of work annually compared to 4.9 for the others. Even medical research seems to favor the affluent—its major triumphs have been over acute, not chronic, disorders.

Medical care, as we know it now, is closely linked with the advancing organization, complexity, and maturity of our society and the increasing education, urbanization, and need for care of our people. Among the results: Medicine is increasingly practiced in hospitals in metropolitan areas.

The relatively few dispensaries for the poor of yesteryear have been supplanted by great numbers of outpatient hospital clinics. These clinics and services are still not adequate—which is why the continuing cry for reform is "more and better." But even when medical services *are* readily available to the poor, they are not used as much as they could and should be. The reasons fall into two categories:

—factors in the present organization of medical care that act as a brake on giving quality care to everyone;

—the life styles of the poor that present obstacles even when the brakes are released.

The very massiveness of modern medical organization is itself a hindrance to health care for the poor. Large buildings and departments, specialization, division of labor, complexity, and bureaucracy lead to an impersonality and an overpowering and often grim atmosphere of hugeness. The poor, with their meager experience in organizational life, their insecurity in the middle class world, and their dependence on personal contacts, are especially vulnerable to this impersonalization.

Hospitals and clinics are organized for "getting work done" from the staff point of view; only infrequently are they set up to minimize the patient's confusion. He fends for himself and sometimes may even get lost when sent "just down the corridor." Patients are often sent for diagnostic tests from one service to another with no explanations, with inadequate directions, with brusque tones. This may make them exceedingly anxious and affect their symptoms and diagnosis. After sitting for hours in waiting rooms, they become angry to find themselves passed over for latecomers—but nobody explains about emergencies or priorities. They complain they cannot find doctors they really like or trust.

When middle-class patients find themselves in similar situations, they can usually work out some methods of "beating the system" or gaining understanding that may raise staff tempers but will lower their own anxieties. The poor do not know how to beat the system. And only very seldom do they have that special agent, the private doctor, to smooth their paths.

Another organizational barrier is the increasing professionalism of health workers. The more training and experience it takes to make the various kinds of doctors, nurses, technicians, and social workers, the more they become oriented around professional standards and approaches, and the more the patient must take their knowledge and abilities on trust. The gaps of communications, understanding, and status grow. To the poor, professional procedures may seem senseless or even dangerous—especially when not explained—and professional manners impersonal or brutal, even when professionals are genuinely anxious to help.

Many patients complain about not getting enough information; but the poor are especially helpless. They don't know the ropes. Fred Davis quotes from a typical poor parent, the mother of a polio-stricken child:

Well they don't tell you anything hardly. They don't seem to want to. I mean you start asking questions and they say, "Well, I only have about three minutes to talk to you." And then the things that you ask, they don't seem to want to answer you. So I don't ask them anything any more. . . .

For contrast, we witnessed an instance of a highly educated woman who found her physician evasive. Suddenly she shot a question: "Come now, Doctor, don't I have the same cancerous condition that killed my sister?" His astonished reaction confirmed her suspicion.

Discrimination also expresses itself in subtle ways. As Frank Riessman and Sylvia Scribner note (for psychiatric care), "Middle class patients are preferred by most treatment agents, and are seen as more treatable. . . . Diagnoses are more hopeful. . . ." Those who understand, follow, respond to, and are grateful for treatment are good patients; and that describes the middle class.

Professional health workers are themselves middle class, represent and defend its values, and show its biases. They assume that the poor (like themselves) have regular meals, lead regular lives, try to support families, keep healthy, plan for the future. They prescribe the same treatment for the same diseases to all, not realizing that their words do not mean the same things to all. (What does "take with each meal" mean to a family that eats irregularly, seldom together, and usually less than three times a day?)

And there is, of course, some open bias. A welfare case

worker in a large Midwestern city, trying to discover why her clients did not use a large, nearby municipal clinic more, described what she found:

Aside from the long waits (8 a.m. to 1 p.m. just to make the appointment), which perhaps are unavoidable, there is the treatment of patients by hospital personnel. This is at the clinic level. People are shouted at, ridiculed, abused, pushed around, called "Niggers,'" told to stand "with the rest of the herd," and in many instances made to feel terribly inferior if not inadequate. . . . This . . . was indulged in by personnel other than doctors and nurses. . . .

Even when no bias is intended, the hustle, impersonality, and abstraction of the mostly white staff tend to create this feeling among sensitive and insecure people: "And I do think the treatment would have been different if Albert had been white."

The poor especially suffer in that vague area we call "care," which includes nursing, instructions about regimens, and post-hospital treatment generally. What happens to the lower class patient once released? Middle class patients report regularly to their doctors who check on progress and exert some control. But the poor are far more likely to go to the great, busy clinics where they seldom see the same doctor twice. Once out they are usually on their own.

Will the poor get better care if "more and better" facilities are made available? I doubt it. The fact is that they underutilize those available now. For instance, some 1963 figures from the Director of the Division of Health Services, Children's Bureau:

In Atlanta, 23 percent of women delievered at the Grady Hospital had had no prenatal care; in Dallas, approximately one-third of low-income patients receive no prenatal care; at the Los Angeles County Hospital in 1958, it was 20 percent; at the D.C. General Hospital in Washington, it is 45 percent; and in the Bedford Stuyvesant section of Brooklyn, New York, it is 41 percent with no or little prenatal care.

Distances are also important. Hospitals and clinics are usually far away. The poor tend to organize their lives around their immediate neighborhoods, to shut out the rest of the city. Some can hardly afford bus fare (much less cab fare for emergencies). Other obstacles include unrealistic eligibility rules and the requirement by some hospitals that clinic patients arrange a blood donation to the blood bank as a prerequisite for prenatal care.

Medical organization tends to assume a patient who is educated and well-motivated, who is interested in ensuring a reasonable level of bodily functioning and generally in preserving his own health. But health professionals themselves complain that the poor come to the clinic or hospital with advanced symptoms, that parents don't pay attention to children's symptoms early enough, that they don't follow up treatments or regimens, and delay too long in returning. But is it really the fault of whole sections of the American population if they don't follow what professionals expect of them?

What are the poor really like? In our country they are distinctive. They live strictly, and wholeheartedly, in the present; their lives are uncertain, dominated by recurring crises (as S. M. Miller puts it, theirs "is a crisis-life constantly trying to make do with string where rope is needed"). To them a careful concern about health is unreal—they face more pressing troubles daily, just getting by. Bad health is just one more condition they must try to cope—or live—with.

Their households are understaffed. There are no servants, few reliable adults. There is little time or energy to care for the sick. If the mother is ill, who will care for her or take her to the clinic—or care for the children if she goes? It is easier to live with illness than use up your few resources doing something about it.

As Daniel Rosenblatt and Edward Suchman have noted: The body can be seen as simply another class of objects to be worked out but not repaired. Thus, teeth are left without dental care. . . . Corrective eye examinations, even for those who wear glasses, are often neglected. . . . It is as though . . . . blue-collar groups think of the body as having a limited span of utility; to be enjoyed in youth and then to suffer with and to endure stoically with age and decrepitude.

They are characterized by low self-esteem. Lee Rainwater remarks that low-income people develop "a sense of being unworthy; they do not uphold the sacredness of their persons in the same way that middle-class people do. Their tendency to think of themselves as of little account is . . . readily generalized to their bodies." And this attitude is transferred to their children.

They seek medical treatment only when practically forced to it. As Rosenblatt and Suchman put it: "Symptoms that do not incapacitate are often ignored." In clinics and hospitals they are shy, frustrated, passively submissive, prey to brooding, depressed anxiety. They reply with guarded hostility, evasiveness, and withdrawal. They believe, of their treatment, that "what is free is not much good." As a result, the professionals tend to turn away. Julius Roth describes how the staff in a rehabilitation ward gets discouraged with its apparently unrehabilitatable patients and gives up and concentrates on the few who seem hopeful. The staffs who must deal with the poor in such wards either have rapid turnover or retreat into "enclaves of research, administration, and teaching."

The situation must get worse. More of the poor will come to the hospitals and clinics. Also, with the increasing use of health insurance and programs by unions and employers, more will come as paying patients into the private hospitals, mixing with middle class patients and staff, upsetting routines, perhaps lowering quality—a frightening prospect as many administrators see it. As things are going now, relations between lower-income patients and hospital staff must become more frequent, intense, and exacerbated.

It is evident that the vicious cycle that characterizes medical care for the poor must be broken before anything can be accomplished.

In the first part of this cycle, the poor come into the hospitals later than they should, often delaying until their disorders are difficult to relieve, until they are actual emergency cases. The experiences they have there encourage them to try to stay out even longer the next time—and to cut the visits necessary for treatment to a minimum.

Second, they require, if anything, even more effective communication and understanding with professionals than the middle class patient. They don't get it; and the treatment is often undone once they leave.

What to do? The conventional remedies do help some. More money and insurance will tend to bring the poor to medical help sooner; increased staff and facilities can cut down the waits, the rush, the tenseness, and allow for more individual and efficient treatment and diagnosis.

But much more is required. If the cycle is to be broken, the following set of recommendations must be adopted:

☐ Speed up the initial visit. Get them there sooner.

☐ Improve patient experiences.

☐ Improve communication, given and received, about regimens and treatment to be followed.

☐ Work to make it more likely that the patient or his family will follow through at home.

☐ Make it more likely that the patient will return when necessary.

☐ Decrease the time between necessary visits.

This general list is not meant to be the whole formula. Any experienced doctor or nurse, once he recognizes the need, can add to or modify it. An experience of mine illustrates this well. A physician in charge of an adolescent clinic for lower-income patients, finding that my ideas fitted into his own daily experience, invited me to address his staff. In discussion afterward good ideas quickly emerged:

☐ Since teen-age acne and late teen-age menstrual pain were frequent complaints and the diagnoses and medications not very complicated, why not let nurses make them? Menstruating girls would be more willing to talk to a woman than a man.

☐ Patients spend many hours sitting around waiting. Why not have nursing assistants, trained by the social worker and doctor and drawn from the patients' social class, interview and visit with them during this period, collecting relevant information?

Note two things about these suggestions: Though they do involve some new duties and some shifting around, they do not call for any appreciable increase of money, personnel, or resources; and such recommendations, once the need is pointed out, can arise from the initiative and experience of the staff themselves.

Here in greater detail are my recommendations:

Increased efforts are needed for early detection of disease among the poor. Existing methods should be increased and improved, and others should be added—for instance, mobile detection units of all kinds, public drives with large-scale educational campaigns against common specific disorders, and so on. The poor themselves should help in planning, and their ideas should be welcomed.

The schools could and should become major detection units with large-scale programs of health inspection. The school nurse, left to her own initiative, is not enough. The poor have more children and are less efficient at noting illness; those children do go to school, where they could be examined. Teachers should also be given elementary training and used more effectively in detection.

Train more sub-professionals, drawn from the poor themselves. They can easily learn to recognize the symptoms of the more common disorders and be especially useful in large concentrations, such as housing projects. They can teach the poor to look for health problems in their own families.

The large central facilities make for greater administrative and medical efficiency. But fewer people will come to them than to smaller neighborhood dispensaries. Imperfect treatment may be better than little or no treatment; and the total effectiveness for the poor may actually be better with many small facilities than the big ones.

Neighborhood centers can not only treat routine cases and act to follow up hospital outpatients, but they can also discover those needing the more difficult procedures and refer them to the large centers—for example, prenatal diagnosis and treatment in the neighborhoods, with high-risk pregnancies sent to the central facilities. (The Children's Bureau has experimented with this type of organization).

There must be better methods to get the sick to the clinics. As noted, the poor tend to stick to their own neighborhoods and be fearful outside them, to lack bus fare and domestic help. Even when dental or eye defects *are* discovered in schools, often children still do not get treatment. Sub-professionals and volunteers could follow up, provide transportation, bus fare, information, or babysitting and housecare. Block or church organizations could help. The special drives for particular illnesses could also include transportation. (Recent studies show that different ethnic groups respond differently to different pressures and appeals; sub-professionals from the same groups could, therefore, be especially effective.)

Hours should be made more flexible; there should be more evening and night clinics. Working people work, when they have jobs, and cannot afford to lose jobs in order to sit around waiting to be called at a clinic. In short, clinics should adapt to people, not expect the opposite. (A related benefit: Evening clinics should lift the load on emergency services in municipal hospitals, since the poor often use them just that way.)

Neighborhood pharmacists should be explicitly recognized as part of the medical team, and every effort be made to bring them in. The poor are much more apt to consult their neighborhood pharmacist first—and he could play a real role in minor treatment and in referral. He should be rewarded, and given such training as necessary—perhaps by schools of pharmacy. Other "health healers" might also be encouraged to help get the seriously ill to the clinics and hospitals, instead of being considered rivals or quacks.

Lower-income patients who enter treatment early can be rewarded for it. This may sound strange, rewarding people for benefiting themselves—but it might bring patients in earlier as well as bring them back, and actually save money for insurance companies and government and public agencies.

Hospital emergency services must be radically reorganized. Such services are now being used by the poor as clinics and as substitutes for general practitioners. Such use upsets routine and arouses mutual frustrations and resentments. There are good reasons why the poor use emergency services this way, and the services should be reorganized to face the realities of the situation.

Clinics and hospitals could assign agents to their lower-income patients, who can orient them, allay anxiety, listen to complaints, help them cooperate, and help them negotiate with the staff.

Better acccountability and communication should be built into the organization of care. Much important information gets to doctors and nurses only fortuitously, if at all. For instance, nurses' aides often have information about cardiac or terminal patients that doctors and nurses could use; but they do not always volunteer the information nor are they often asked, since they are not considered medically qualified. This is another place where the agent might be useful.

It is absolutely necessary that medical personnel lessen their class and professional biases. Anti-bias training is virtually nonexistent in medical schools or associations. It must be started, especially in the professional schools.

Medical facilities must carefully consider how to allow and improve the lodging of complaints by the poor against medical services. They have few means and little chance now to make their complaints known, and this adds to their resentment, depression, and helplessness. Perhaps the agent can act as a kind of medical ombudsman; perhaps unions, or the other health insurance groups, can lodge the complaints; perhaps neighborhood groups can do it. But it must be done.

Treatment and regimens are supposed to continue in the home. Poor patients seldom do them adequately. Hospitals and clinics usually concentrate on diagnosis and treatment and tend to neglect what occurs after. Sometimes there is even confusion about who is supposed to tell the patient about such things as his diet at home, and there is little attempt to see that he does it. Here again, follow-up by sub-professionals might be useful.

Special training given to professionals will enable them

to give better instructions to the poor on regimens. They are seldom trained in interviewing or listening—and the poor are usually deficient in pressing their opinions.

Clinics and hospitals could organize their services to include checking on expatients who have no private physicians. We recommend that hospitals and clinics try to bring physicians in poor neighborhoods into some sort of association. Many of these physicians do not have hospital connections, practice old-fashioned or substandard medicine—yet they are in most immediate contact with the poor, especially before hospitalization.

Medical establishments should make special efforts to discover and understand the prevalent life styles of their patients. Since this affects efficiency of treatment, it is an important medical concern.

I strongly recommend greater emphasis on research in medical devices or techniques that are simple to operate and depend as little as possible on patient's judgment and motivation. Present good examples include long-term tranquilizers and the intrauterine birth-control device which requires little of the woman other than her consent. Such developments fit lower-class life style much better than those requiring repeated actions, timing, and persistence.

As noted, these recommendations are not basically different from many others—except that they all relate to the idea of the vicious cycle. A major point of this paper is that equal health care will not come unless all portions of that cycle are attacked simultaneously.

To assure action sufficiently broad and strong to demolish this cycle, responsibility must also be broad and strong.

□ Medical and professional schools must take vigorous steps to counteract the class bias of their students, to teach them to relate, communicate, and adapt techniques and regimens to the poor, and to learn how to train and instruct sub-professionals.

□ Specific medical institutions must, in addition to the recommendations above, consider how best to attack all segments of the cycle. Partial attacks will not do—medicine has responsibility for the total patient and the total treatment.

□ Lower-class people must themselves be enlisted in the campaign to give them better care. Not to do this would be absolutely foolhardy. The sub-professionals we mention are themselves valuable in large part because they come from the poor, and understand them. Where indigenous organizations exist, they should be used. Where they do not exist, organizations that somehow meet their needs should be aided and encouraged to form.

□ Finally, governments, at all levels, have an immense responsibility for persuading, inducing, or pressuring medical institutions and personnel toward reforming our system of medical care. If they understand the vicious cycle, their influence will be much greater. This governmental role need not at all interfere with the patient's freedom. Medical influence is shifting rapidly to the elite medical centers; federal and local governments have a responsibility to see that medical influence and care, so much of it financed by public money, accomplishes what it is supposed to.

What of the frequently heard argument that increasing affluence will soon eliminate the need for special programs for the poor?

□ Most sociologists agree that general affluence may never "trickle down" to the hard-core poverty groups; that only sustained and specialized effort over a long period of time may relieve their poverty.

□ Increased income does not necessarily change life styles. Some groups deliberately stand outside our mainstream. And there is usually a lag at least of one generation, often more, before life styles respond to changed incomes.

In the long run, no doubt, prosperity for all will minimize the inferiority of medical care for the poor. But in the long run, as the saying goes, we will all be dead. And the disadvantaged sick will probably go first, with much unnecessary suffering.

May 1967

The Strange Case
of Public Dependency

MARTIN REIN

A famous violinist once told Groucho Marx that he had supported himself since the age of five. "What were you before that," Groucho demanded to know, "a bum?"

All of us, even concert violinists, are dependent during major and important periods of our lives. No one finds this strange or reprehensible. What does cause great, and rising, concern is public dependency—even though it may apply to the same periods, and even sometimes to the same persons.

This conception of dependency as a social evil is in part the legacy inherited from the early English Victorians. It is deeply ingrained in our philosophy of individualism and our commitment to industrialism. The critical social problem in the early nineteenth century was "pauperism," a condition defined as individual weakness of character which "poor relief" only encouraged. Nor have we today resolved the moral dilemma posed in the Victorian era. The fear that economic security robs initiative and promotes dependency

169

is an abiding and disturbing issue in contemporary social policy.

In a period of unprecedented prosperity, with the predicted Gross National Product for 1965 almost 660 billion dollars, three very different factors intensify public concern over dependency: rising welfare costs, obtrusiveness of the urban poor, and rising unemployment.

The Social Security Administration estimates that the total spent on health, welfare, and education during fiscal 1963-64 was 71 billion dollars. This exceeds the total outlay for national defense. Today about 12 percent of the Gross National Product is spent on social welfare. When public and private costs are taken together, expenditures exceed 108 billion dollars. The unrelenting rise in public assistance expenditures (which in the public mind is identified with the dole) worries critics even more than the total cost. Expenditures for public aid (including medical payments and other programs) more than doubled in the past decade and a half, rising from approximately two-and-a-half billion dollars in 1949-50 to more than five-and-a half billions in 1963-64. But the critics seldom note that public aid expenditures as a percentage of Gross National Product remained unchanged at .9 percent, and the per capita cost increased less than almost every other kind of social welfare expenditure.

More than 220,000 families have been displaced by "urban renewal" in the last fourteen years. This does not include those moved for "public improvements"—public housing, parks, highways, public buildings, code reinforcement. It is estimated—and estimates are usually conservative—that the next decade will see close to a million persons displaced.

Two-thirds of those uprooted by renewals have been Negro. Their ability to move in the city and to find suitable low cost homes is limited. Their plight has been graphically described as a black neck caught in a white suburban noose. Uprooted and transported, they have suddenly become prominent and visible.

They have been wrenched from their protective sub-cultures and exposed to the standards of a more demanding society. Chester Hartman, research fellow at the MIT-Harvard Joint Center for Urban Studies, after an extensive review of the literature on relocation concludes that "the deleterious effects of the uprooting experience, the loss of familiar places and persons, and the difficulties of adjusting to and accepting new living environments may be far more serious issues than are changes in housing status." Those who are relocated may experience a greater sense of personal failure and have less ability to cope with their environment. A program intended to aid the poor may unintentionally serve to increase their dependency.

Unemployment continues high. Recovery from each recession finds it at a higher level than the preceding recession. Our traditional institutions seem unable to cope with our growing labor force and the technologically displaced. The private sector of the economy has had in the past five years a growth rate which has absorbed less than half of the increase in the labor force. Some critics believe that we are in danger of producing in the future a social underclass, displaced victims of a society which no longer requires their labor and rejects them as useless.

Like our Victorian predecessors we want to reduce dependency (pauperism), and like them we tend to see it in individual and personal terms, a form of social pathology. We prescribe social services for those receiving public financial aid; rehabilitation to make slum dwellers more acceptable tenants; and training programs to make them more employable. But in our attempts to reduce these dependencies we neglect the idea that those receiving public aid have a right to adequate and decent levels of assistance.

We tend to ignore the amount of low income housing actually available to the poor; and we neglect the development of policies to expand industries and services which can contribute jobs for the unskilled.

But what actually is dependency? What assumptions do we hold about it?

☐ We believe that the dependents among us can be isolated and identified as somehow morally and socially, if not physically, less adequate human beings than the rest of us.

☐ We believe dependency would disappear if only we would eliminate the personal inadequacies of the dependents themselves.

☐ We believe dependency is bad. We must work to reduce it.

Here is the popular dichotomy: those who give and those who receive; those who take out of our economic system more than they put into it, and those who pay the difference. Broadly speaking, those who work or have wealth are considered to contribute more than they get. If these ideas shed light on little else, they do illustrate how our social thinking is tied to the ethic that the "improvident" poor have somehow brought their ills upon themselves.

Each of these assumptions warrants re-examination.

I believe it far more profitable to view economic dependence as biologists view ecologic dependence: we are all involved with one another. Life is interdependent—and the most fruitful understanding of it can come from examining degrees and conditions of interdependency, rather than from isolating debits and credits in a ledger which draws a dichotomy between the dependent and the independent.

Over time, as well as at any moment, man is both dependent and independent. The two states are closely related. After an age when most mammals have passed into senility or death, man is still dependent, still undergoing the long training in education, socialization, and skills he needs to function adequately; and as society grows more complex the process of maturation takes longer and longer.

We all experience dependency at some time. Childhood, schooling, illness, old age, pregnancy, child-birth, and early child-rearing all include periods of dependency. Few people now believe that these dependencies are undesirable. Few argue that we don't need more well-trained physicians, scientists, and humanists, even though this means that many adults will not "produce" until they are thirty. We believe that the social benefits—the "total production" —are well worth the temporary costs. Obviously then, not all dependency can be bad.

Generally, we are trying to extend socially desirable dependency to more and more people. Barbara Wootton has perceptively observed that economists make dizzy leaps between two rival assumptions about social dependency:

First, the doctrines of scarcity economics (which have the merit of being agreeable to common sense) teach that thrift and work are the keys to prosperity: the longer and the harder everyone works, the better will it be for all. Then, with the swing to economics of depression, common sense is abandoned in favor of the paradox that it is not saving but spending, not working but withdrawal from work, which conduces to economic health.

Many professionals believe that if we only knew what bothered the individual, and applied the right remedy to him, then we might be able to take him completely out of dependency and make him a right thinking, wealth-producing, tax-paying (rather than tax-eating) citizen, to use President Johnson's recent terminology.

No two schools agree on the exact composition of that elixir. Some favor a get-tough policy (Newburgh, New York), others prefer a more humanistic and therapeutic approach, stressing indivudual rehabilitation (1962 amendments to the Social Security Act). Both views share a common assumption, that the dependent has an inadequate personality—a position which has been correctly described by Peter Marris as "fundamentally arrogant." This approach has, nevertheless, been made virtually the sole basis of many therapeutic professions. Dependency as well as poverty may not be the result of personal inadequacy nearly so much as it is the result of the structure of society.

If dependency is a fault of individual personality, and the dependent is a less adequate person, then the third common assumption follows inevitably: dependency is bad —let's get rid of it. However, if we view dependency in terms of social organization rather than individual pathology, we arrive at different social judgments and treatments.

Dependency is fundamental to life, part of its basic fabric. We must concentrate on its patterning and expansion, not regard it merely as an area of rot which must be cut out or at least "contained." It has long term causes and long term effects, and they must be analyzed. We need to develop a language of social growth and social costs, comparable to the concepts of individual growth and individual pathology.

No act is, after all, without its consequences, no social act without its social costs. We often pay dearly for what seemed like a good policy at the time—and may even have been a necessity. Such socially unanticipated consequences —or "disservices"—greatly affect the amount and direction of dependency. They are the costs of progress.

According to William K. Knapp, writing on *The Social Costs of Private Enterprise,* economic disservices include "all direct and indirect losses suffered by persons or the general public as a result of economic activities." The costs of extra washing and of respiratory troubles from industrially polluted air are such disservices as are other hazards to health and safety caused by business and industry. Often the organization of the market does not require a business to pay the economic cost to others of its actions. In the same way, the social costs of technological change are not borne by those who benefit most directly.

We neglect these disservices partly because we tend to regard industrialization in a society much as we regard puberty in a youth—we assume that once it is technically past it is all over, and growing up and adjusting is finished. Actually the tensions and problems associated with growth continue at each stage of development.

In the early stages of industrialization almost all other interests of our society were subordinated to it. It left a toll of human suffering so severe and widespread that, according to Karl Polanyi, if unchecked, it could have wiped out civilization. With the movement from farm to industrial town came overcrowded slums, gross exploitation of labor, the brutalization of work, a declining standard of living (at least in the short run), and the incalculable psychological suffering as the centuries' old way of life broke down. Richard Titmuss notes: "Most of the long-industrialized countries of the West are still burdened by the as yet uncompensated disservices of the early stage of their economic growth."

We are hindered by the new adjustments rising from what George Friedman calls "making industrial man into an object of rationalized production." Close to a quarter billion tests are given annually to determine how well we can be made to fit into the increasingly specialized tasks of business and industry. All this testing and adjusting is going ahead despite the fact that, as a recent Russell Sage Foundation report says, "virtually nothing is known at present about the impact the testing movement is having on the society as a whole . . . (or) the individuals . . . directly affected."

Tests increase "rationality" and "objectivity." Many

executives and educators welcome the chance to reduce the unpredictability of personality to scores on a profile or holes in a card.

But those tested are not as enthusiastic. As one passes through the sorting process, his chances for work, education, status, fulfillment, and even social benefits are determined by a new form of social discrimination, most potent against those already disadvantaged. The reject will likely respond by retreating—turning his back on what he is not "fit" to obtain. A recent proposal has urged a United States Supreme Court test of the constitutionality of determining the educational future of children of underprivileged backgrounds through the use of intelligence and aptitude tests. "Selection for excellence" is therefore becoming an increasingly effective way to create dependents.

Another potent multiplier of dependency is automation. This is becoming an old, much documented story. In the last decade the population of the United States increased by 20 percent, production increased 43 percent, but the number of factory workers decreased 10 percent. We will need twelve million new jobs in the next decade—at present rates, which may decline, we supply six.

It is not because our economy is not working well (as during the depression) that these people become dependent —but because it *is* working well. Efficiency has made them superfluous or branded them incompetent. They did not pass the tests; they had the wrong skills or backgrounds; they were too old; they were in the wrong place; they could not adapt quickly enough. They no longer fit and are rejected. Technical progress increases dependency.

While industry often informs a man that he is too old to be hired at forty, medicine informs him that he can expect to live past seventy. A white girl born in 1959 has a better chance of reaching age sixty than her grandmother, born in 1900, had of reaching age five. Should that grandmother, however, still be alive, she can look forward to another sixteen years. The aged population is increasing rapidly.

The young, too, are fruitful and multiply. Posperity breeds optimism; prosperous women breed babies. More people marry, they marry younger, they have children earlier. Enough babies are born each year in the United States (and live past infancy) to populate Chicago, plus a couple of its suburbs. The young and old make up our two largest and most rapidly growing groups of dependents. Like the universe we are exploding in all directions.

And not only are the traditional killers of the very old and very young being overcome; we provide sheltered environments in which the deprived, rejected, handicapped, weak, and sick survive longer. We seldom make them well and competent (our illness patterns have shifted from acute to chronic)—we merely help them live longer. If anything, it has made them more dependent than before. Medical progress increases dependency.

Social disservices also occur in education and welfare— where social consequences are supposed to be anticipated. For instance, many believe that the best way to "anticipate" and "prevent" trouble is by early diagnosis and intensive treatment, but individuals singled out for such treatment often find themselves stigmatized and discriminated against—precisely what the treatments were supposed to prevent—and the programs boomerang. In England, epileptics avoid treatment for this reason—employable before "help" which labels them, they are often not employable after. In New York *potential* delinquents may find themselves bearing the onus of *actual* delinquents—and react accordingly. We are affected in what we are by the way others see us. Human behavior comes to conform with the assumptions we make about it. Labelling increases dependency.

We rehabilitate and retrain ex-convicts, ex-mental patients, and the unemployed to be able to hold jobs and fit into our society. We do not retrain industry, unions, government, or people generally to accept them. We run the risk of not delivering what we promise. Programs aimed solely at changing individuals and which neglect institutional reforms must encounter this difficulty.

The Job Corps as organized remains a splintered and isolated program; unless positive steps are taken to assume that its graduates really get more jobs or education or social and health services, it will have little effect. Established programs tend to stubbornly resist integration with new resources, and this contributes to one of the gravest deficiencies in these community programs. There is danger in starting a cycle of social change for which we provide no closure.

The higher the expectation, the greater and more complete the disappointment and feelings of hopelessness, worthlessness, and cynicism so characteristic of the American poor. The greater the leap between aspiration and reality, the more inevitable that fall. We may succeed in imbuing lower-class people with middle-class standards of success; and thereby do little more than deprive them of the supports of lower-class life.

The Job Corps, like all retraining programs, must decide whom to take and whom to reject. To assure the success and continued congressional support of this controversial program, a substantial amount of "creaming" may be unavoidable—accepting those who need the program least, but are most likely to succeed. But what will be the meaning for those who are turned away? What explanations will be offered to those not accepted? Titmuss has recently suggested that rejection from the Job Corps may mean ultimate rejection from the world of work, and this may prove to be more important than rejection by the armed forces, the colleges, or employers in business and government. And if we fail to provide those who have been rejected with physical and mental health services, we also exclude them from the world of clinical help. We thus assign them to a form of social death—scrap them as "social junk," to use Park's graphic term.

We give capital depletion allowances and pursue other policies resulting in the use of labor-saving devices and the reduction of low skilled jobs. But, for the most part we do not create national policies which encourage the development of labor-intensive industries such as health, nursing, education, recreation, and welfare—vital to the poor themselves as services. Shortages in these fields could be partly met if those jobs which needed less training were filled by those who had less training. But the people who take such jobs must feel that they have futures and can rise eventually to professional status. Little organized effort is being made to reduce the rigidities of procedure which block this upward mobility. Professional associations, as well as labor unions, attack it as a threat to "quality of service" and to professional privilege and position. Retraining and professionalism themselves contribute to dependency.

Since success is increasingly determined by who can get, or has, an education, future failures are being created earlier and earlier—and with less and less chance of reprieve. This trend is intensifying.

Not all failures come from lack of ability; a very great many are socially determined. Some persons never get adequate opportunities for education or training; others do not want—or do not know how—to take advantage of them. Alfred J. Kahn, professor at the New York School of Social Work, sums up:

> Of every one hundred children of high school age, eighty-seven enter high school and sixty-seven graduate . . . only thirty enter college and fifteen are graduated.

. . . Of school drop-outs, one of three leaves during the eighth grade or before. . . .

More than two-thirds of all children complete high school, but only 45 percent of poor children; 30 percent of youth on Aid to Families of Dependent Children (age 18-24) had not completed high school. Nor is the situation improving. A recent national survey dismally notes: "Little, if any, gain has been realized in the proportions of ADC children finishing high school since (a comparable) 1950 study was completed." Eighty-nine percent of the bright sons of the well-to-do expect to go to college, but only 29 percent of the brightest sons of the poor. Among dullards (those with lowest quintile I.Q. scores) 56 percent of the prosperous expect college, but only 9 percent of the poor even hope for it. Intentions must be distinguished from action. When actual enrollments rather than expectations are examined, the picture is even worse. Moreover, there is a strong and continuous trend downward—almost 1 in 4 heads of poor families have even less education than their parents, if those parents had nine grades or more—despite the urgent necessity for more education than the previous generation. The final grim shadow for the future is cast by the 1965 report of the Council of Economic Advisers:

Many individuals fail to develop their talent fully, often for economic reasons. In 1970, one third of the top 25 percent of youth did not go on to college; 5 percent did not even finish high school. This is a serious waste.

The uneducated are even more handicapped in the search for jobs today than they were two decades ago. Since the median educational level of the entire male labor force has risen by more than 50 percent, the dramatic and disturbing results are clear. Today one third of all Negro youth age 16-21 who are out of school are also out of work.

A dropout who finds a job is, of course, "independent" early, and some might rejoice at this fact. But as a national survey shows, dependency increases soon, and greatly: 57 percent of dropouts under twenty-five were unemployed during the last five years, compared to 4 percent of college graduates.

The much-heralded theory of the poverty cycle assumes that poverty is self-perpetuating because deprivation in one generation leads, through cultural impoverishment, to family breakdown and indifference to educational achievement of children, to poverty in the next generation. A valid alternative analysis would focus not on personal defects but on institutional rejection, and the indifference which leads to development of protective subcultures which wall people off from the threatened destruction of their personalities.

Economic poverty begets educational poverty which begets economic poverty which begets dependency which begets economic and educational poverty—in a continuous closed circle of "begets." Children of poor parents study in larger classes with more difficult students in schools with less money under teachers who are paid less and are less well trained. Their education is inferior and they are little motivated or encouraged.

The rejects from our various selection processes form an army of outcasts, the socially disaffiliated. England has its "teddy boys," Russia its "hoodlums," and we our delinquents and skid row bums. All countries have "problem families."

Our rising affluence increases the army of those who prosper and belong; it also creates a permanent underclass who suffer from deprivation, failure, and loss of status.

What happens to the "socially disaffiliated?" According to sociologist Erving Goffman in his article, "Cooling the Mark Out," we create social ghettos where,

. . . . persons who have died in important ways come gradually to be brought together into a common graveyard that is separated ecologically from the living community. . . . Jails and mental institutions . . . certain regions and towns in California (set aside) as asylums for those who have died in their capacity as workers and as parents, but . . . still alive financially. For the old in America who have also died financially . . . old folks homes and rooming house areas . . .

During a depression a "failure" can blame his plight on the "system"; during prosperity it is much more difficult to avoid blaming himself, and becoming hopeless and apathetic. The ethic of the prosperous—that their welfare is due entirely to their own virtuous efforts—is infecting the poor, in reverse.

How does a society respond to its socially deprived? Some writers, like Talcott Parsons and Bronislaw Malinowski, believe that social systems have built in equilibrium mechanisms that make automatic adjustments to servere threat.

But they tend to ignore the time lag—the years during which much suffering and misery is endured, before "natural counter-forces" can deflect or gear them to useful purposes—if they ever do so.

As we examine the mechanism of response—the social services provided in America's Welfare State—it becomes apparent that there is a curious disregard for those dependents whose plight is most desperate. Two crucial policy questions must be examined: who gets what services? What is the quality of those services? Even a cursory examination of these questions led Gunnar Myrdal to conclude that there is "a perverted tendency" in American social policy so that those who need help most do not get it.

So pervasive has been our failure to cope with poverty and dependency that this tendency can be called the Iron Law of Social Welfare.

□ *Medical care.* James N. Morgan and his colleagues

found in a national study that only one-third of poor families have hospital insurance of minimal adequacy, and three-fifths have no insurance at all. Using disability as a measure of need, only 24 percent of families with a person disabled were covered, compared to 76 percent with no one disabled.

A recent report on the quality of medical care in New York City found that accredited specialists provide different care in different hospital settings. Ability and training alone do not assure quality services. How services are organized and, we expect, to whom they are offered, also affect the quality of care. Physicians consider out-patient clinics the Siberias of hospitals, and serve grudgingly; students and interns are seldom adequately supervised. There are too few physicians, too many sick, too little time, not enough concern for the patient.

□ *Welfare*. Welfare programs are supposed to add to the incomes of those who do not have enough to live decently. But a University of Michigan study showed that half of the families in poverty did not receive any form of transfer payments, including social security. Daniel P. Moynihan, Assistant Secretary of Labor, has recently quipped that "social security is for winners, not losers," meaning those who have won some economic stability. Pensions help even fewer; only 11 percent of the poor had private pension help, compared to 40 percent of all families. Finally, only 23 percent of the poor receive public assisance.

□ *Child care*. The iron law does not make exceptions for the young and weak. Alfred Kahn has recently documented the nature and scope of what he calls our "urban-child care crisis." He calls attention to the long term and sometimes unnecessary institutionalization of children; long term waiting in temporary shelters; frequent shifting of children from foster home to foster home. The handicapped, emotionally damaged, and nonwhite children are those most disadvantaged. The long term consequences of their neglect will be paid in the next generations.

□ *Education and housing* have already been discussed Education is the path upwards—and the poor, down farthest, get the worst, and have least motivation to use what they have. In housing the very large families and the "socially unacceptable" (those with unwed mothers, for instance) are hardest to place.

□ *Mental health*. The most skilled psychiatrists and psychologists have always worked with the least disturbed patients. Treating middle- and upper-class neurotics generally yields better results—and income—than treating lower-class psychotics. One of the reports of the Joint Commission on Mental Health and Illness notes: "Usually the most difficult social and psychological problems fall in the area of no one's responsibility. The psychotics, sexual psychopaths, persons with suicidal or homicidal impulses, and persons presenting acute somatic symptoms are the groups left without any help short of commitment."

Is the Iron Law of Social Welfare really iron—that is, inevitable? If so why?

I believe that the three chief factors that lead to denial of services to those in greatest need are professionalization, the rejection or inability of the needy to use the services, and the logical consequences of our social philosophy.

Professionals want to get satisfaction, pleasure, prestige, status, and income for their work. They want their efforts to succeed and to be acknowledged and appreciated. The most difficult, suspicious, recalcitrant, ignorant, impoverished, and hopeless cases afford little opportunities for such satisfactions.

We need more knowledge about the professions which are "increasingly becoming the arbiters of our welfare fate." Titmuss notes that, "We have to ask . . . questions about the ways in which professional people (doctors, teachers, social workers, and many others) discharge their roles in diagnosing need and in selecting and rejecting patients, clients, and students for this or that service."

Professional associations will not readily pose these questions because they are organized by professionals themselves to serve their own interests. Change usually must come from outside, but often in cooperation with insurgent insiders. The public health movement rose over the vigorous opposition of physicians; and the juvenile courts developed in spite of lawyers, not because of them.

The poor and the dependent may be even less eager to work with professionals than the professionals are to work with them. Despite their physical presence in our cities they live in a far country with its own iron laws, which we must learn. As voluntary consumers of social services they will not willingly do things merely because respectable people think they should, nor deliberately seek out what looks like trouble or embarrassment. The barriers they create to social reformers are, as Herbert Gans has pointed out, "reaction (s) to the threat of humiliation,"

Professional and organizational commitment must precede the demand for responsibility, cooperation, motivation, and trust. Consumer rejection is most likely to be overcome only when we offer authentic programs with assured delivery, rather than promissory notes.

Our social philosophy states strongly that the greatest rewards should go to the most productive. "Who does not work, neither shall he eat." Those who do not produce are by implication, inferior. Our humanitarian values (no one should starve in the midst of plenty) may seem to be contradicted; nevertheless we increasingly demand of the needy that they be willing to conform and be "rehabilitated" from the sin of dependency to qualify for financial aid.

Many so-called welfare payments, like social security,

are in fact rewards or delayed payments for productivity, not really welfare at all. Returns are related to earned salary; benefits are channeled through the wage system; the marginal groups follow the iron law and are excluded. When liens on property are required to qualify for public assistance, aid really becomes a temporary loan. One early reason given was ease of administration: the stable and employed are easy to handle and find. Another is the "foot in the door" tactic: it is felt to be politically sounder to establish a welfare principle with socially acceptable groups, and then hope coverage and benefits trickle down. But the trickle-down system has not always worked. For example, from its very inception workman's compensation was restricted to the aristocracy of the manual workers— the skilled laborer. Even today, 20 percent of workers, concentrated among the unskilled, are not covered. We often find it inexpedient to accept our social services for what they are. For instance educational programs of great national benefit appear coyly—and with inadequate coverage— behind the fig leaves of "GI Bills" for veterans or national defense scholarships.

In broad summary:

□ Our present welfare policy is not really designed to reach the neediest.

□ The poor have their own defenses against imputations of inferiority, and they resist assimilation.

□ Professionalization has hindered work with the poor.

To repeal the iron law we must develop social philosophy and techniques specifically designed for that purpose. We have the choice—the dilemma is one of ideology not technology.

Social welfare is a means to an end—and it is within our power and privilege to choose both the means and the end. Bismarck used social welfare to perpetuate an empire; in the thirties the United States used it to prevent social disruption. Today we employ it to preserve the middle-class ethic of rewarding the industrious.

We can continue along this path, or we can make welfare serve social justice and humanitarianism by using the criterion of common citizenship, in which need, not virture determines aid. If we choose the former, we had better think seriously about whether we really want to end the problems of dependency at all.

If we really mean to attack dependency:

☐ Redistribution of income and benefits must be the fundamental principle which informs our social policy. We must invest much more work and money, absolutely and relatively, for the underprivileged. Post-hospital care, expanded job and educational opportunities—such services must be available to all of the poor.

☐ Teachers, social workers, doctors, and others who choose to work with the poor, instead of being in effect penalized financially for their choice, should be given special rewards and incentives—including much more recognition.

☐ When we think of the dependency of the poor, our attention is rigidly fixed on those who should be working and are not. We neglect the student preparing for a socially useful occupation, the mother caring for children, the aged who have earned retirement, the workers who are forced out of the labor force by technological change. We do not reject dependency—only dependency of the poor.

We need to extend the principles of socially accepted dependency to the poor. We also need to raise the "acceptable" school-leaving age, lower retirement age, and provide for periodic retraining. Dependency must become a social right which can expand freedom, and increase the range of human choice. Such a policy could well decrease future dependency and make old age less terrifying.

In the twentieth century, we may witness as dramatic a

change in social policy direction as the shift from pauperism poverty in the preceding century. We must in the next era develop policies based on: socially accepted forms of dependency; adequate rather than minimum services; compensation for those disadvantaged by rapid technological change. Such policies must be informed by a philosophy of redistributive social justice.

What would such a program look like? *The Economist,* a pragmatic scholarly journal in England, has proposed programs for the radical reform of the social services. *The Economist* divided social services into two distinct objectives: 1) generous compensation for those damaged by rapid economic change; 2) a separate program for the relief of need. In specifics:

☐ *Unemployment pay* should be increased so substantially that, for a short time, a man thrown out of a job should actually get more than he did while on the job to compensate for the pain in looking for a new job.

☐ *Mustering out pay* (or pension) for men displaced by technological change, to be drawn for short periods (five years) even after they accept other jobs.

☐ *Housing subsidies* to be attached to tenants rather than to houses—that is, a redistribution of subsidies to people rather than to structures.

☐ *Income guarantees* unrelated to previous wages earned, so that the retired can maintain a standard of living much higher than known during their working years; an income consistent with the changing standard of living resulting from economic growth which will permit the poorest section of the old-age population to maintain a decent and adequate standard of living without recourse to public assistance.

☐ *A graduated social security tax* which would be sharply progressive and have an income redistributive effect.

☐ *Higher family allowances*, even above the guaranteed income level (or the prevailing wage scale), for poor parents with very large families.

The politics of who gets what and how, outside of the market, will become the salient issue of our vast social services in the generations to come. Solutions to the problem of dependency will be found only as we develop a social calculus which acknowledges our social costs and a constituency which can, in this new political game, make its weight felt to help pay them. We must search out, as Titmuss has recently suggested, "ways of extending the welfare state to the poor."

March/April 1965

NOTES ON CONTRIBUTORS

Lilyan Binder   "Becky and the Telegraph Avenue Scene"

Has been associated with the Berkeley Rap Center, involved with staff development and training. She is currently with the Community Mental Health Program, School of Social Welfare, Berkeley, specializing in youth involvement, alienation and drug abuse.

Claire Brady   "Becky and the Telegraph Avenue Scene"

Received her M.S.W. degree from the School of Social Welfare, University of California, Berkeley in June 1970. Her major interest has been in psychiatric casework particularly with young people. She plans to work with a community mental health center in the San Francisco Bay Area.

Sandra Broemel   "Becky and the Telegraph Avenue Scene"

A recent M.S.W. from the School of Social Welfare, University of California, Berkeley. She continues to be concerned with providing services for the Telegraph Avenue population.

Susan Cady   "Becky and the Telegraph Avenue Scene"

Received her M.S.W. degree from the University of California, Berkeley, School of Social Welfare in June 1970. During the past year and a half she helped organize the Telegraph Avenue Concerns Committee and the Berkeley Free Clinic for youth not cared for by existing services.

Robert Coles   "The Case of Hugh McCaslin"

Research psychiatrist at Harvard University. Coles has worked in Appalachia and as a consultant to the Appalachian Volunteers. He has published widey in the field of child psychiatry and is the author of several books including *Children of Crisis: A Study of Courage and Fear*.

William H. Friedland   "Labor Waste in New York:
                          Rural Exploitation and Migrant Workers"

Professor of community studies and sociology at the University of

California at Santa Cruz. He is author of *African Socialism* and co-author (with Irving Louis Horowitz) of *The Knowledge Factory*.

Estelle Fuchs   "How Teachers Learn to Help Children Fail"

Associate professor at the Education Foundations Department of Hunter College in New York City. She is author of *Pickets at the Gates* and *Teacher Talk: Views Inside City Schools*, from which this article was taken.

Nathan L. Gerrard   "The Serpent-Handling Religions of West Virginia

Professor and chairman of the department of sociology, Morris Harvey College, Charleston, West Virginia. He has had nine years of contact with the serpent handlers and other rural, non-farm poor in West Virginia. He and his wife are preparing a manuscript on the rural folk of West Virginia and he is the author of a chapter in a forthcoming book on Appalachia to be published by the University of Pittsburgh.

Robert Hart   "Becky and the Telegraph Avenue Scene"

Received his M.S.W. from the University of California, Berkeley, School of Social Welfare in June 1970. He is currently employed at the State Hospital in Mendocino, California as a psychiatric social worker.

Oscar Lewis   "The Culture of Poverty"

Professor of Anthropology at the University of Illinois. He has conducted family studies in Mexico, New York and Puerto Rico, and most recently in Cuba. Among his books are: *Five Families, The Children of Sanchez; Pedro Matinez: A Mexican Peasant and His Family;* and *La Vida: A Puerto Rican Family in the Culture of Poverty—San Juan and New York.*

Walter B. Miller   "White Gangs"

Research associate at the Massachusetts Institute of Technology-Harvard University Joint Center for Urban Studies. A Member of the Subcommittee on Research of the National Manpower Advisory Committee, he is an anthropologist.

Ann Ohren   "Becky and the Telegraph Avenue Scene"

The former assistant administrator of the Berkeley Community Clinic, she received her M.S.W. in community organization and administration in March 1970 and is now working part time at the Berkeley Rap Center and part time on transforming the larger report on Telegraph Avenue life styles into book form.

Marc Pilisuk   "Becky and the Telegraph Avenue Scene"

Professor in residence, School of Social Welfare, University of California, Berkeley. (For more detail see the back cover.)

Phyllis Pilisuk   Introduction

M.S. in sociology from the University of Michigan. Currently enrolled in the School of Social Welfare, University of California at Berkeley. (For more detail, see back cover.)

David Pittman   "Homeless Men"

Professor of sociology and director of the Social Science Institute of Washington University. He has published widely in the area of social deviancy with particular emphasis upon alcoholism, drug addiction, criminology and sexual deviance. Among his works are *Revolving Door: A Study of the Chronic Police Case Inebriate*.

Martin Rein   "The Strange Case of Public Dependency"

Professor of social policy at the Massachusetts Institute of Technology. Rein is presently studying changes in social security policy in the United States, Sweden and England. His books include *Social Policy: Issues of Choice and Change* and *An Assessment of Strategies to Reduce Poverty*.

William Smolak   "Becky and the Telegraph Avenue Scene"

A psychiatric consultant to the Probation Department of Sonoma County, California. He has worked with adolescents in family treatment in encounter groups; he received his M.S.W. from the University of California, School of Social Welfare in June 1970.

Anselm L. Strauss   "Medical Ghettos"

Professor of sociology and chairman of the graduate program in sociology at the University of California Medical Center in San Francisco. He is author of several books on problems of health care and treatment, and issues surrounding the medical profession including *The Professional Scientist* and *Boys in White*.